Paper Airplanes That Really Fly!

Fighter Jets

by Andrew Dewar

PERIPLUS

Contents

What's in This Book, and Where You'll Find It

Part One: Flaming Jets, Flying Sculpture

- 4 Flaming Jets, Flying Sculpture
- 5 The Quest for Greater Speed
- 6 Early Jets
- 7 The Different Approaches of Parsons and Coanda
- 8 British Jets
- 9 Fledgling Jets
- 10 Jet Basics
- 11 Centrifugal and Axial Jets
- 12 German Jets
- 13 Revolutionary Jets
- 14 Jets Over Korea
- 15 Sabre versus MiG
- 16 Going Supersonic
- 17 New Fuselage Shapes
- 18 Saab's Jets
- 19 Viggen, Draken and Gripen
- 20 The Arrow Conspiracies
- 21 The Arrow's Destruction
- 22 Century Series
- 23 Sleek New Designs
- 24 X-Planes
- 25 Exotic Jets
- 26 Vertical Jets
- 27 The Hawker Harrier
- 28 Skunk Works
- 29 Spy Planes
- 30 Stealth Jets
- 31 Drastic Design Changes
- 32 Jets on Display

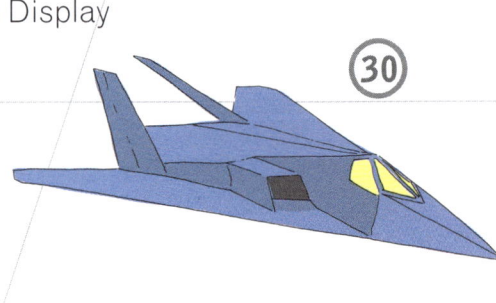

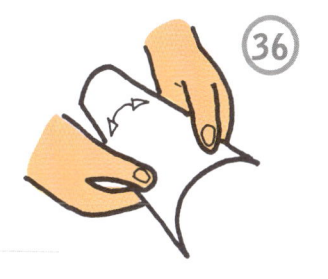

Part Two: Assembly Instructions

34 Building and Flying Fifteen Paper Jets
36 General Instructions and Flying Tips
42 Jumpjet
44 Hornet
45 Kingfisher
46 Vulcan
48 Lockheed P-80 Shooting Star
50 Messerschmitt Me 262
52 North American F-86 Sabre
53 Scimitar
54 Northrop B-49
56 Avro CF-105 Arrow
57 Saab Draken
58 Lockheed F-104 Starfighter
60 Northrop F-5 Tiger
62 Grumman X-29
63 Lockheed F-117 Nighthawk
64 Fly Your Planes!

Part Three: Fifteen Airplane Kits

65 Jumpjet
67 Hornet
69 Kingfisher
71 Vulcan
73 Lockheed P-80 Shooting Star
75 Messerschmitt Me 262
77 North American F-86 Sabre
79 Scimitar
81 Northrop B-49
85 Avro CF-105 Arrow
87 Saab Draken
89 Lockheed F-104 Starfighter
91 Northrop F-5 Tiger
93 Grumman X-29
95 Lockheed F-117 Nighthawk

Flaming Jets, Flying Sculpture

We live in the jet age, and we think of jets as the epitome of modern technology. Jets mean new and powerful. But in fact, jets have been flying for more than half the history of heavier-than-air flight. The very first jets flew before the Second World War, and came of age during the Korean War. They are hardly new.

The Spitfires and Mustangs of World War II had hit a developmental wall. No matter how much power was added they couldn't go any faster. Their wings created too much drag, and their propeller tips were spinning faster than the speed of sound. They vibrated dangerously, and sometimes they broke apart.

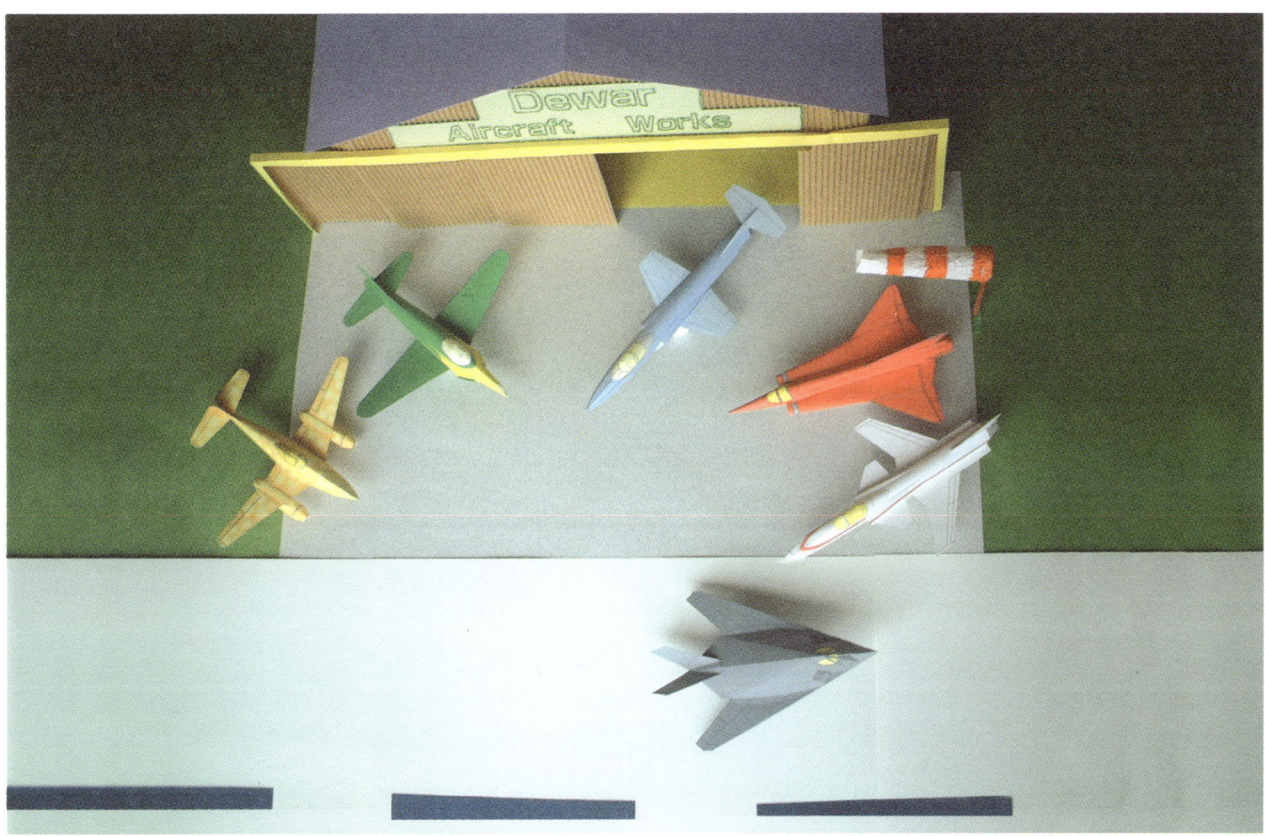

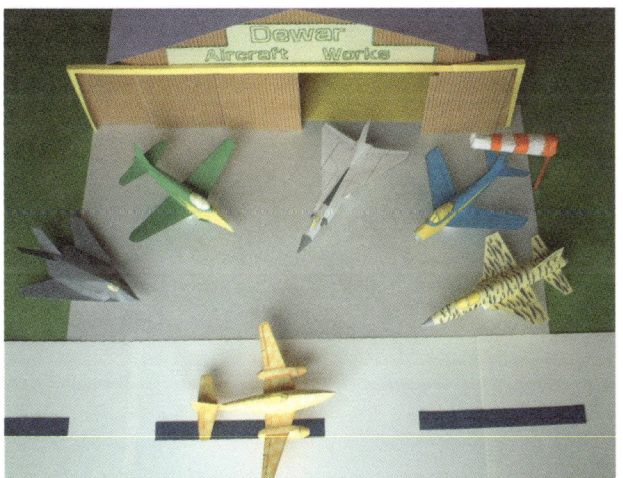

The Quest for Greater Speed

The future of the airplane was in speed, so a new engine was needed to push them higher and faster. The jet engine was the answer, and the jet fighter was born. Fighter jets have a kind of functional beauty I have always liked, so I have chosen some of my favorite planes for paper models. I prefer not to think of them as weapons, but rather as flying sculpture, and so I have given most of them airshow colors. And I have written not about their feats of war, but the fascinating stories of how they came to be built.

Real jets fly high and fast, and so do these. Be sure you have lots of room when you go flying, and don't take your eyes off them!

Early Jets

By the beginning of World War II, fighter planes were reaching their speed limits. The faster they flew, the more drag held back the plane. The fastest fighters might need twice as much power to add even a few miles per hour to their speed.

Then a new problem arose. If pilots dived their planes too fast the plane began to shake violently, lose lift, and even become uncontrollable. The stick would freeze, as if fixed in cement, and the plane would crash. It wasn't clear why this happened, and no one knew how to solve the problem. It was called compressibility, because the air seemed to be unable to get out of the way of the plane! Mustangs, Hellcats, and especially Lightnings had do-not-exceed speed limits, but the limits were different for different altitudes, because they were based on the plane's critical Mach number, the speed at which compressibility began. Critical Mach numbers were easy to forget in a dogfight, and many planes and pilots were lost.

The speed of sound changes according to the temperature and pressure of the atmosphere. At sea level, where the air is relatively warm and dense, the speed of sound is 760 mph (1,216 kmh), but at 37,000 feet (11,312 m, a little above where jumbo jets usually fly), the cold thin air reduces the speed of sound to about 660 mph (1,056 kmh). So because the speed of sound isn't a constant number, it is referred to as Mach 1 (after Ernst Mach, who pioneered research into it). Half the speed of sound is Mach 0.5, and twice is Mach 2.

Some airplanes, like the later model Spitfires, were able to dive to much higher speeds. The Spitfire's thin wing and slim fuselage gave it a critical Mach number of 0.9, which means it could dive to nine-tenths of the speed of sound without danger.

Then a new problem arose. The tips of the propellers were spinning faster than the speed of sound and losing their effectiveness. It seemed as though fighters had reached their absolute limit. But fighter pilots needed even more speed, and piston engines didn't have enough power to provide it. Some new kind of engine was needed.

The Different Approaches of Parsons and Coanda

In 1884, Charles Algernon Parsons built a steam turbine to create electricity. Instead of pushing a piston, the high-pressure steam turned a kind of propeller, which spun the generator. The turbine was both light and powerful, and so he thought it might be applied to a ship. He built the *Turbinia* to try his engine, and tested it in 1894. But the propeller was unable to absorb the energy of the engine. Parsons redesigned the propellers (increased to three), and in February 1896 drove the *Turbinia* to an unheard-of 32.75 knots.

Parsons' steam turbine was an early form of jet engine, using a jet of high-pressure steam to create mechanical energy. A large part of the success of the *Turbinia* was due to its tiny size, and the fineness of its hull (it was extremely narrow for its length), but the steam turbine was useful for many kinds of ships, and is still used today. It is interesting to note that the huge passenger liner *Mauretania* could have been powered by just two of the jet engines used in the latest jet fighter, the X-35.

The *Turbinia* in front of the *Mauretania*

Rumanian pioneer Henri Coanda took a different approach. He used a 50 horsepower reciprocating engine to turn a centrifugal compressor inside a tight cowl. The jet of air blown back by the compressor powered the plane he built to hold it, a sleek plywood-covered biplane finished in 1910. Coanda's *turbo-propulseur* would not have been powerful enough to get the plane airborne, but many years later Coanda claimed to have added fuel to the jet to increase the thrust, and crashed just after takeoff. But if he really had burned fuel, he would have been sitting amidst the flames…

The Caproni-Campini N.1 worked on the same basic principle as Coanda's unsuccessful jet. An ordinary piston engine drove a compressor, which blew compressed air at high speed through a variable area nozzle to provide thrust. Fuel was burned behind this in a kind of afterburner to give additional thrust, though in fact it added only about 28 mph (45 kmh) to the basic speed of 205 mph (328 kmh). And the engines drank fuel at such a rate that when the plane was flown from Milan to Rome (a distance of 169 miles (270 km)) in 1940, it had to stop at Pisa to refuel.

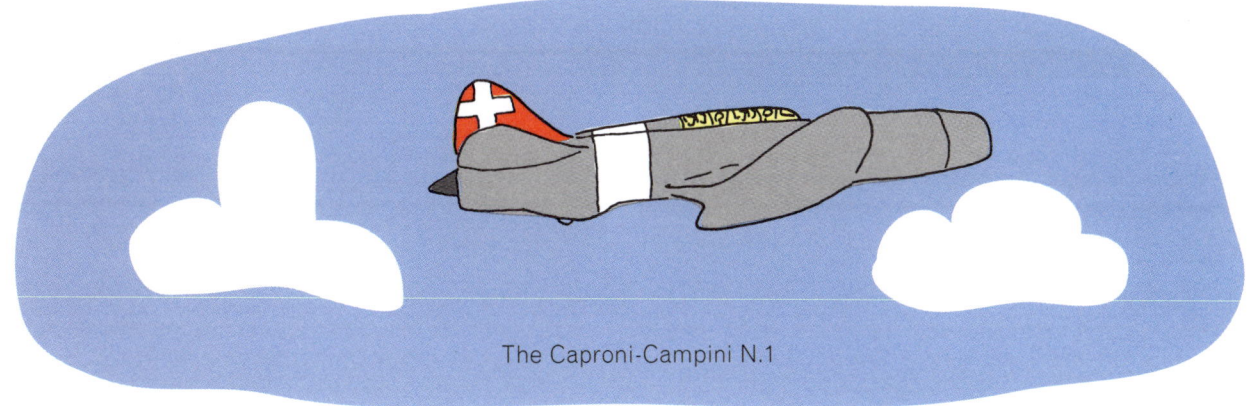

The Caproni-Campini N.1

 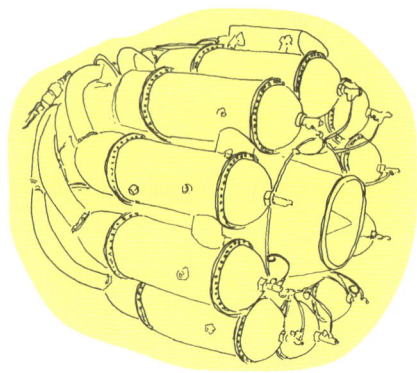

British Jets

The inspiration for a truly practical jet engine came to Frank Whittle while he was a Royal Air Force College cadet, writing about *Future Developments in Aircraft Design* in 1928. The airplanes of the time did well to reach 150 mph (240 kmh), but Whittle thought a new kind of engine, one in which a compressor was turned by a gas turbine, would make it possible to fly up to 500 mph (800 kmh) at altitudes where propellers would no longer be useful. He patented his idea in 1930, but lacked the money to either build it or renew his patent. In 1935, however, the Air Ministry agreed to let Whittle develop a prototype, and he formed his company Power Jets to build it. He struggled with breaking turbine blades, engine surges, and overheating, but by 1937 the determined Whittle had a working engine. It was far from perfect, but it was much lighter than piston engines of the same power.

This is the engine that first flew in the Gloster E.28/39. The Whittle W.1 had 860 pounds (390 kg) of thrust.

The Whittle W.1's 860 pounds (390 kg) of thrust were equivalent to about 688 horsepower. This meant that the Gloster jet's 300 mph (480 kmh) performance was matching that of many frontline fighters on half the power! And later, with a new engine, the E.28/39 flew even faster, to 466 mph (746 kmh).

The Gloster E.28/39 itself was never intended as anything more than a research aircraft, but its high speed and excellent handling immediately suggested a jet fighter. Gloster Aircraft was at work on a new design even before the first test plane flew. George Carter knew that one engine would not provide enough power for a fighter, and after long thought put an engine in each wing. The first prototype flew on 13 November 1943, and by July 1944 the first production Gloster Meteors had reached RAF squadrons and seen action. And with engine and airframe changes, the Meteor remained in frontline service for more than ten years.

An airplane was needed to test the engine, and Gloster Aircraft was contracted to build it. Designer George Carter watched the engine running, noted the expected thrust, and sharpened his pencil. And on 15 May 1941 it lifted off (much to the relief of the staff pilots, who half expected the new type of engine to wriggle around like a dropped garden hose) and became the world's third jet aircraft to fly. Those who flew it remarked on the smoothness.

Heinkel He 178

Heinkel He 280

Fledgling Jets

Meanwhile, in Germany, Pabst von Ohain was developing a similar type of engine. Neither man knew of the other's work, but von Ohain enjoyed better financial support, and no doubt was helped by being unknown to the German Air Ministry as well. Once he had a 1,100 pound (500 kg) thrust centrifugal engine running, Ernst Heinkel built the tiny He 178 to test it. With the retracting wheels locked down and the wheel wells fared over, the He 178 began taxi trials, and on 27 August 1939 it became the first jet aircraft in history to fly. In later tests it reached 435 mph (696 kmh), but even after World War II began the Air Ministry remained unimpresssed.

with 1,650 pound (750 kg) jet engines its performance was at best unremarkable. Early test flights were conducted in secret, but the Airacomet was occasionally spotted by practicing fighter pilots, who were amazed to see a plane flying quite comfortably without any sign of a propeller!

Convair XP-87

Early jets used fuel at such a huge rate they were useless for bomber escort duties. The U.S. tried several combination designs, with a piston engine at the front for cruising, and a jet engine at the back for combat. But the jet engine was dead weight when not in use, and drag from the propeller held back the jet. The Convair Vultee XP-81 was one of these, but it lost out to the pure jet P-80 and the piston engined P-82 Twin Mustang.

Bell XP-59 Airacomet

When the Air Ministry finally took notice of the jet engine, they agreed to let Heinkel develop a fighter aircraft to go with the engine. The result was the twin-engined He 280, which in addition to its engines was unusual in having a tricycle landing gear and a pressurized cockpit. The first version flew as a glider with ballast in dummy nascelles, and later flew with the engines uncowled on 2 April 1941. But though the He 280 could beat the best piston fighter in mock dogfights, better planes were already on the way, and it never saw use.

The first jet to fly in the United States was the Bell XP-59 Airacomet. It was designed from the beginning to become an operational fighter, and had two 1,300 pound (590 kg) thrust General Electric 1A engines (which were Americanized Power Jets W.2Bs, developed by Whittle). 65 Bell P-59s were ordered, and the first flew on 1 October 1942, but even when reengined

Britain developed one more jet fighter during the war, to join the classic Meteor. This was the de Havilland Vampire, made of wood and powered by de Havilland's own Ghost engine. The Vampire not only became an international bestseller, but was transformed by successive changes in wing and engine into a supersonic fighter.

de Havilland Vampire

Jet Basics

A balloon can become a jet, if you blow it up and let it go. A jet is essentially a spray of any kind of fluid, but for now let's just think of air. You know what happens when you let the balloon go. Although it spurts around in all directions, it is pushed forward as air rushes out of the open nozzle. But it is not air pushing against air that powers the jet. A balloon would buzz around just the same way in a vacuum. The reason is that the high-pressure air inside the balloon is pushing against the rubber sides, trying to expand, but it is resisted on all sides except one: the side opposite the nozzle, where the leaking air is meeting no barrier. Without anything to balance it, the air pushing the rubber wall opposite the nozzle pushes the whole balloon with it.

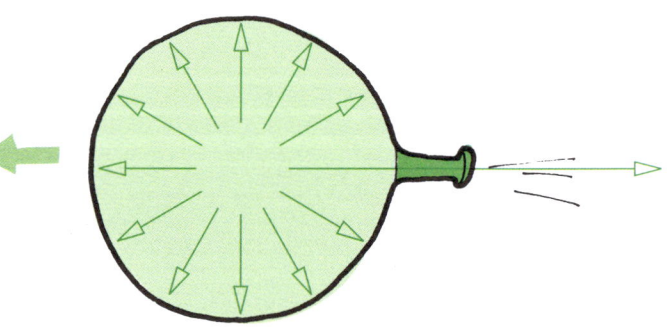

Heron of Alexandria, a Greek mathematician and inventor who was active around 62 A.D., invented a small toy that ran by steam and might be called the first steam engine. A flame under the water resevoir made steam, which built up pressure and passed through the side pipes into the ball at the top, and then out through the two bent nozzles. The jets of steam, or rather the equal and opposite reaction to them working on the nozzles, turned the ball at high speed. Although this was just a toy, it could be made to turn other devices and do work.

The first jet engine to be tried in an airplane was Coanda's ducted fan. Here is how it works. Air flows into a large cowl and is compressed by a fan. The fan is driven by an ordinary piston engine, and it compresses the air by throwing it to outwards towards the cowl by centrifugal force. When this compressed air tries to expand, it can only flow backwards, and this creates a forward push on the engine. As Coanda built it, the ducted fan does work, but is no more efficient than an ordinary propeller. If fuel is added to the compressed air and burned, the air tries to expand much more quickly, resulting in much more thrust.

The simplest kind of pure jet is the ramjet. Ramjets have no moving parts, and are only limited in their maximum speed by the ability of their materials to withstand the tremendous heat and stress from air friction at high Mach numbers. Cool air is captured by the large inlet at the front of the engine and compressed by the constriction in the middle. The air tries to resist, but is rammed through by fresh air coming in behind. When the air is quite compressed, fuel is added and burned, and the hot expanding gasses gush out the opening at the back, pushing the engine. There is one big problem, however. Ramjets won't start unless they are already travelling at high speed, so some other kind of engine is needed for takeoff and acceleration.

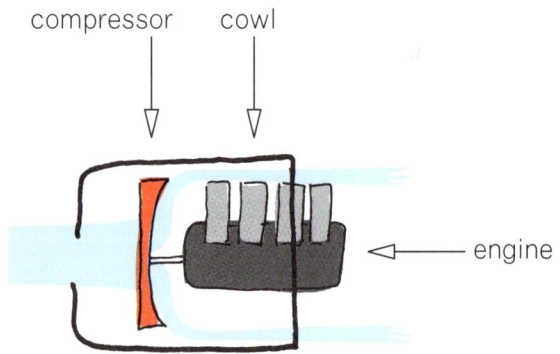

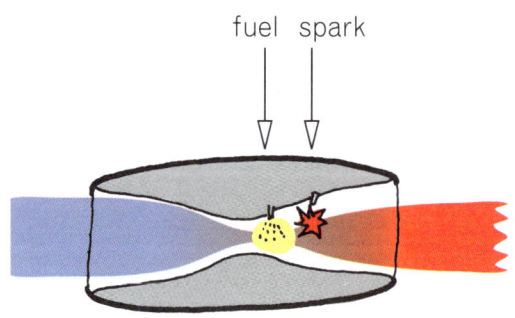

Centrifugal and Axial Jets

The first turbojets, jets using turbines, were developed in Britain by Frank Whittle and in Germany by Pabst von Ohain at almost the same time. Both were centrifugal jets. Cool air coming into the engine through the inlet hits a fan and is compressed by centrifugal force. This high-pressure air is forced into the burner cans arranged around the outside of the engine, where fuel is added and burned. The hot gasses rush out the back through a turbine, which turns like a pinwheel and drives the compressor fan in the front. Centrifugal jets are relatively simple to build and very robust, but a lot of power is lost because of the two right angle turns the air must make.

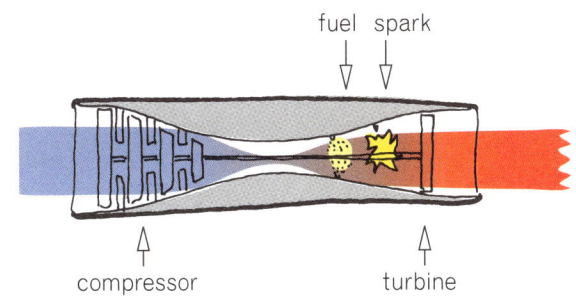

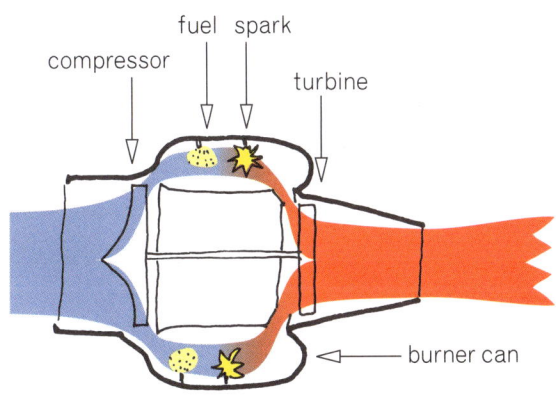

The next big step in jet development was the axial flow turbojet. Instead of pushing the air to the outside and making it turn tight corners at high speed, the axial flow engine allows the air to flow straight through along its axis. Cool air coming in from the inlet hits a series of spinning and stationary compressor fans, which compress it to a very high pressure. Then fuel is added and burned, and the hot gasses rush out the tailpipe past the turbine, which drives the compressor. Another advantage of this layout is that the turbine can be made to drive things other than just the compressor: the propeller in a turboprop plane, the large ducted fan in a jumbo's turbofan engine, or the lift fan in the X-35. In addition, it is much slimmer than the centrifugal jet engine, which allows for slimmer, sleeker airplanes.

If you add an afterburner, in which extra fuel is added to the already hot exhaust gasses, you can increase the power of the engine by a third or more. The afterburner can be used just when needed, for takeoff or combat, and turned off for cruising. But it guzzles fuel, and can really only be used for a few minutes at a time.

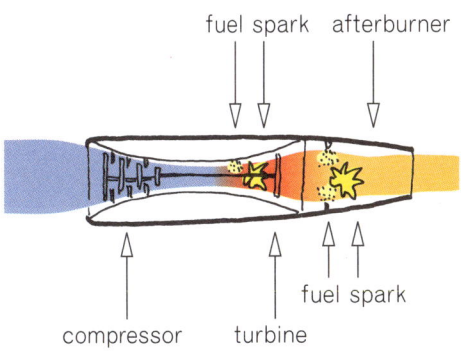

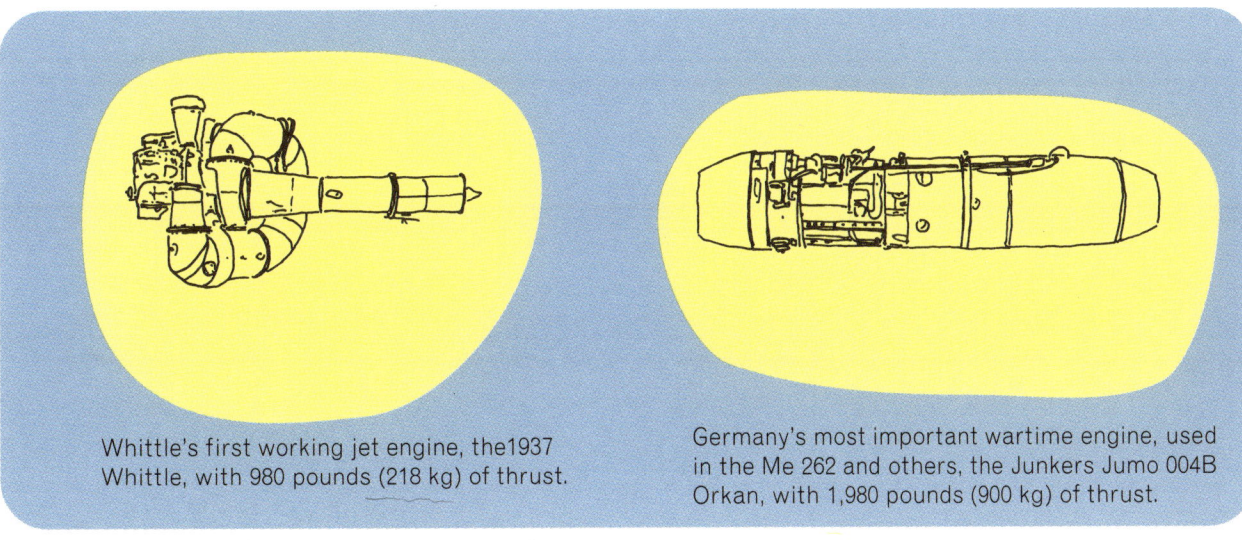

Whittle's first working jet engine, the 1937 Whittle, with 980 pounds (218 kg) of thrust.

Germany's most important wartime engine, used in the Me 262 and others, the Junkers Jumo 004B Orkan, with 1,980 pounds (900 kg) of thrust.

German Jets

The world's first operational jet fighter began rather strangely. Instead of the bulky centrifugal flow jets used in the Heinkels and Glosters, Messerschmitt planned to use revolutionary slim axial flow jets built by Junkers. In order to get the most speed possible out of the airframe, Messerschmitt used very thin swept wings. But the plane was ready before the engines, so the first prototype was flown with a piston engine. It had barely enough power to get off the ground, but it flew. Early versions of the jets were added; this time the jets cut out just after takeoff and the propeller barely got the plane around for a landing. The Me 262 had to wait for a redesign of the jet engines.

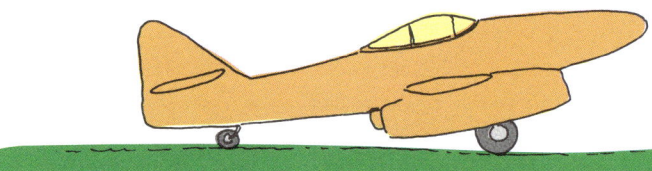

The new jet had many revolutionary features, but tricycle landing gear was not among them at first. Even after the piston engine was replaced with jets, the tailwheel remained. The first attempts to get the third prototype airborne were fruitless, because the tail would not come up. It was in the shadow of the wing and air wasn't reaching it. Test Pilot Fritz Wendel decided to touch the brakes when flying speed was reached, and the shock would lift the tail. It worked, and test flying began. But it was hardly a safe solution, and a nose wheel was added to later prototypes.

It was a lucky thing for the Allies that the German leaders didn't take note of the jet's potential until quite late. It was also lucky that Hitler believed the war would be over in a few months and that no new fighters were needed. Even when the Me 262 was flying and ready for delivery to squadrons, he insisted that it be converted to a bomber. Messerschmitt delayed, hoping Hitler would change his mind, and when he finally did it was far too late for this jet fighter to make much difference in the war. Had it entered combat any earlier, the allied bombers would have had a much, much more difficult time than they did. The Me 262 was a truly great fighter, but its real moment came only after the war, when large numbers were carried back to the U.S. and Russia for study.

Revolutionary Jets

One more jet fighter to see combat in wartime Germany was the remarkable Heinkel He 162 Salamander. Remarkable not because of any exceptional performance, but because it was intended to be a *Volksjaeger*, a "people's fighter" that could be built cheaply of simple materials by semi-skilled labor (or even slave labor). The order went to Heinkel, and less than 90 days later the prototype was flying! Ultimately, the placement of the heavy engine on the back of the wing made lateral stability tenuous, and even very skilled pilots found it dangerous to fly.

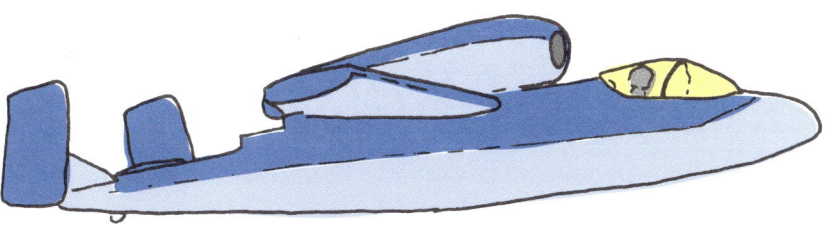

The Horten Ho IX is another jet fighter whose greatest legacy was the inspiration it provided to future designs, in this case Northrop's flying wing bombers. The Horten brothers had been flying all-wing sailplanes for years before the war, and adding jet engines seemed a natural develpment. But only a few flights were squeezed in before the end of the war.

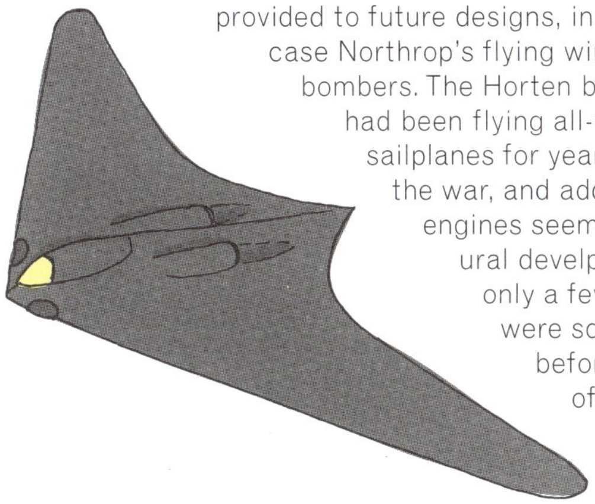

The Germans tried just about everything. This monstrosity is the Junkers Ju 287, built to test the properties of swept-forward wings. Backward-swept wings were necessary for high-speed flight, but unstable at landing speeds; forward sweep was expected to solve that problem. The Ju 287 was patched together from bits of other planes with new wings and four jet engines, and showed that the theory was right, but in practice the wing often wanted to twist itself off.

Many other revolutionary jets were being designed and built when the war ended. Some look modern even today. They show the breadth and depth of German aerodynamic research, and provided inspiration for many later American and Soviet fighters.

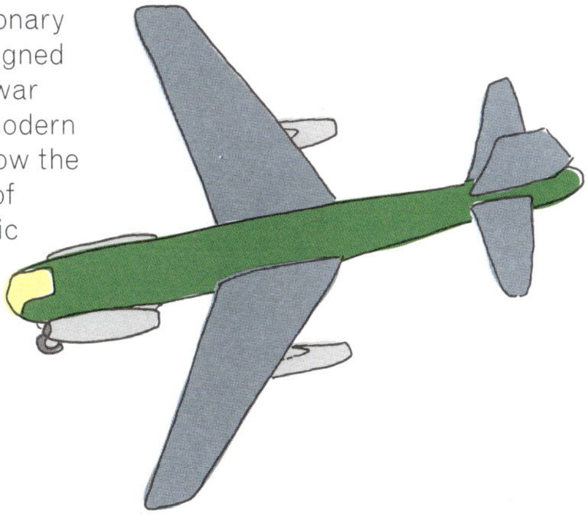

Blohm und Voss P.212-03

The Focke-Wulf Ta 183 was nearly ready to fly at the end of the war. It is clearly the inspiration for the MiG-15.

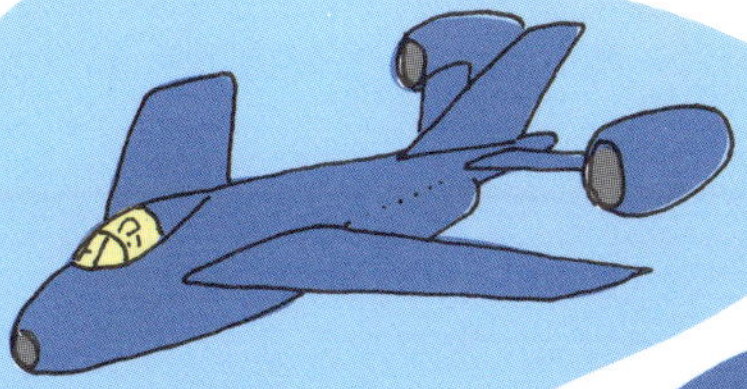

Heinkel P.1080

Focke-Wulf Ta 283

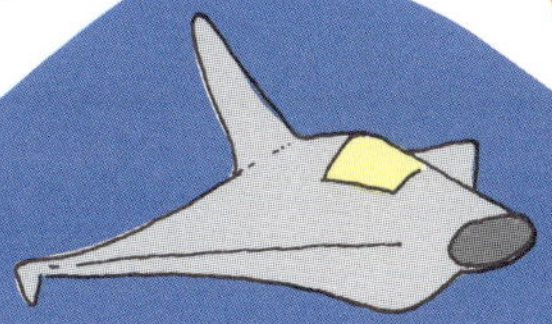

Lippisch P.12

Henschel P.135

Jets Over Korea

Just five years after the end of World War II, the great nations were back at war. But this time the alignments had changed: communism versus democracy. The new battlefield was Korea, split in two along the 38th parallel, with forces backed by a China that had just turned red on the northern side, and a south supported by the U.S. and Britain.

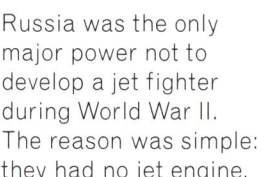

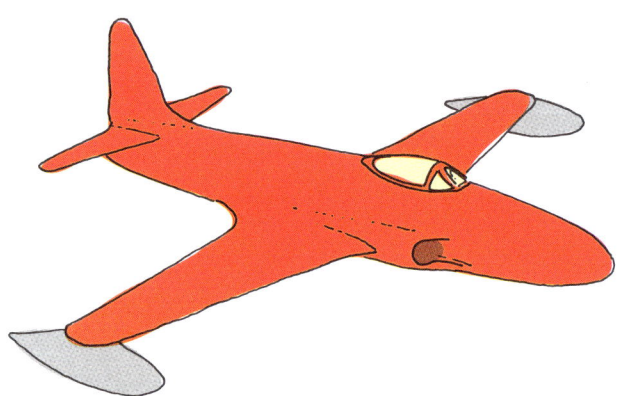

Russia was the only major power not to develop a jet fighter during World War II. The reason was simple: they had no jet engine.
Then someone made a very big mistake. Despite general distrust of the Soviet Union after the war, the British exported a Rolls-Royce Nene engine to Russia. Soviet engineers immediately reverse engineered it and made copy after copy...

At the beginning of the war both sides flew fighters left over from World War II, with a few new types. Western forces had a few jets: P-80 Shooting Stars, F-84 Thunderjets, and Grumman Panthers for the U.S., CF-100 Canucks for Canada, and Meteors and

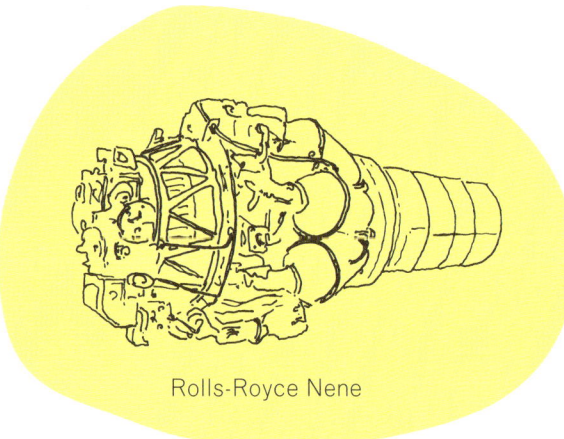

Rolls-Royce Nene

Vampires for the British. But the communist forces started with old piston fighters, and the West felt sure of a quick victory.

The Soviets had something else up their sleeve... At the end of the war they grabbed all the German jets and scientists they could. They found the research on swept wings and learned how to build fighters that could fly at nearly the speed of sound. The result of the marriage of the British Nene with a German-style airframe was the Mikoyan-Gurevich MiG-15. Jets were set to fight jets for the first time ever.

Western forces got a nasty shock when the MiG-15 suddenly showed up over Korea in November 1950. Its swept wings gave it far better performance than the straight-winged jets the allies were flying. MiGs could fly circles around the slower P-80s and Meteors. The West began to lose its grip on the sky.

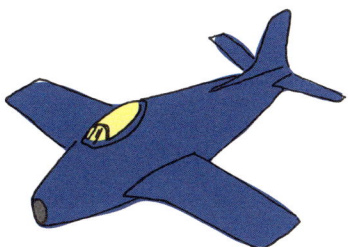 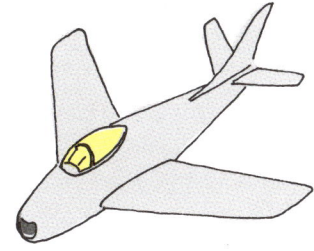

Sabre versus MiG

But the Americans also had German data, and very soon they were adding swept wings to their jets too. North American Aviation took the basic design for their straight-winged FJ-1 Fury, slimmed down the fuselage, and swept the wings and tail to make the first F-86 Sabre.

The sudden appearance of the MiG-15 hurried the decision to use the Sabre in combat. American pilots found that the MiG was a better all-round airplane, but the Sabre was quite good enough for the Allies to put their superior training into play. Still, the pilots wanted even more speed. Even if they had to trade away range and maneuverability, speed was what they wanted. And that meant they wanted a still newer generation of planes, planes that were supersonic.

The Hawker Hunter isn't strictly speaking a Korean War jet, but it belongs to the same era. It's here because it was Britain's most important domestic and export fighter for years, and because many people think it was the most beautiful fighter ever. (Me, I think it was the Spitfire, but my father flew Spits so I might be biased.)

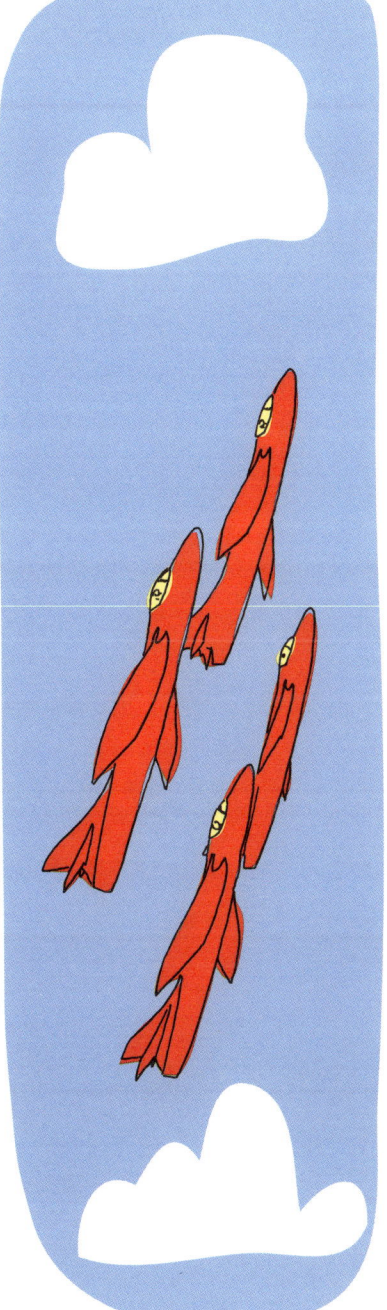

Going Supersonic

Pilots who dove their planes close to Mach 1 encountered extreme drag and a loss of control, and with even occasional break ups. This de Havilland DH 108 research jet may have flown supersonically...but very little was left after the attempt.

In Britain, Miles began working on the M.52 research plane, and intended to use a jet engine and razor thin wings to muscle past the sound barrier. But fears of the dangers to the pilot led to cancellation. And then on 14 October 1947, Chuck Yeager flew the bullet-shaped Bell X-1 rocket plane past Mach 1. The barrier was broken.

Compression occurs as the speed of air, or the speed of something passing through air, approaches the speed of sound. This is because pressure waves (of which sound waves are one kind) cannot travel faster than the speed of sound, and therefore air is unable to get out of the way of approaching obstacles. It becomes uncompressible, and shock waves form. In the case of airplanes, the airflow over the curved wing is faster than the plane's airspeed, and becomes supersonic in places at the plane's critical Mach number (in this example, Mach 0.8). This makes a shock wave which creates huge drag and stalls the back of the wing. When the wing reaches sonic speed (Mach 1.0), there are shock waves on both sides of the wing.

But at supersonic speeds, the shock waves are at the front and back of the wing, and have less effect. Note that at Mach 1.0 the shock waves are just about where control hinges would be, and this is why the controls freeze.

In general, the fatter the wing the more air will accelerate over it. If thick and thin wings are flying at the same speed, the fat wing will develop a shock wave sooner. And it will have more difficulty reaching supersonic speeds.

In prewar Germany, Alexander Lippisch began investigating swept and delta wing shapes. He discovered that the speed of the air across the chord (or width) of the wing, measured at right angles to the leading edge, decreased as the sweep of the wing increased. Since this delayed the onset of shock waves, more sweep meant less drag at higher speeds and a much higher critical Mach number. Or put another way, swept wings made planes faster. Lippisch's research planes were brought to the U.S. and studied carefully. The family resemblance between this Lippisch glider (left) and the Convair XF-92 (right) is clear at a glance.

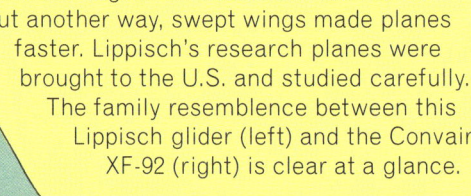

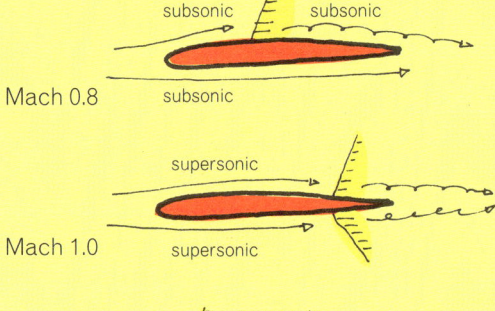

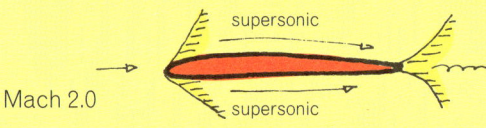

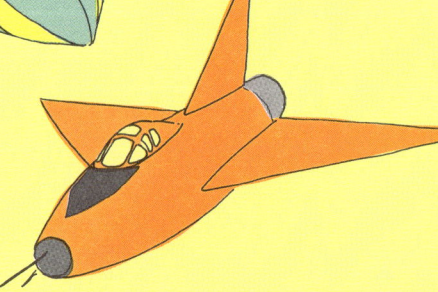

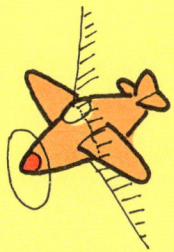 

New Fuselage Shapes

Something similar to the wing shock wave happens with the whole plane, but fatter fuselages will create shock waves at lower speeds than thin ones.

 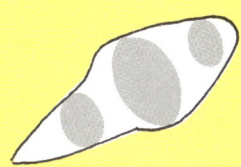

before area ruling   what the air sees

 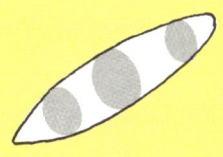

after area ruling   what the air sees

Whitcomb thought that even if the fuselage looked streamlined, the supersonic airflow added the cross-sectional area of the wing to that of the fuselage. This gave the fuselage a huge draggy bulge in the middle that the air couldn't flow around easily. If, on the other hand, the fuselage was slimmed down to offset the area of the wing, the air would see a nice, clean, streamlined-looking body. To the airflow, it would seem as though there was no wing. And so, much less drag.

Whitcomb called it the Transonic Area Rule. The press called it the coke-bottle fuselage.

 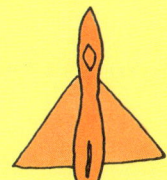

The effect of area ruling is especially clear on the Convair F-102 Delta Dagger. When Convair built the XF-92, they made full use of German high-speed flight research and Dr. Lippisch's advice, and expected the resulting plane to surpass Mach 1. It didn't. Convair's second try was the XF-102, still with a bullet-like fuselage. Before it was finished, Whitcomb's area rule discovery was announced, but Convair stubbornly pushed ahead with their original design. It too failed to go supersonic. When Convair relented, and the F-102 was pinched in the middle according to the area rule, it popped effortlessly through the sound barrier while still climbing. And so jet fighters became supersonic.

Supersonic flight turned out to be more complicated than just fat or thin, straight wings or swept. No matter how thin or how swept the wings, planes were having trouble getting through the sound barrier because of the huge increase in drag. The usual way of dealing with drag would be to steamline the airplane, and give it a nice smooth round shape. But in the case of uncompressible supersonic air, this kind of streamlining didn't work. Then Richard Whitcomb at the Langley Research Center of the NACA (the precursor of NASA) realized what the problem was: the wings had to be counted with the fuselage and steamlined as a whole.

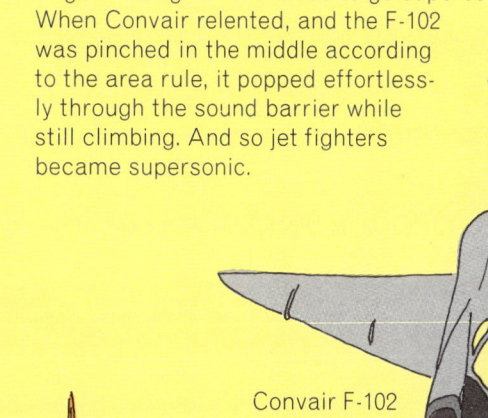

Convair F-102 Delta Dagger

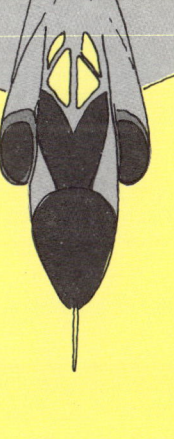

Convair XF-92

Saab's Jets

Sweden has a long history of aviation, and leading up to the Second World War, it had the beginnings of an aircraft industry as well. For many years it had bought airplanes from Germany, Britain, and the United States. But the situation in Europe was becoming uncertain, and if Sweden wanted to maintain its neutrality it would need both strong defences and locally built airplanes. The government took out licenses to build Junkers bombers, Northrop dive bombers, and North American trainers. And the Svenska Aeroplan Aktiebolaget (SAAB), formed in 1937, was given the task of building them.

Saab J 21

Just before the Second World War began, however, the Swedish Defense Minister realized still more planes were needed and asked Saab for help. Saab requested the right to compete equally with foreign manufacturers and export as well. The government agreed, and Saab was given a virtual monopoly on aircraft manufacture.

Saab had built another advantage into the J 21: it could easily be converted to jet power. Work began in 1945, and though the new J 21R had to be 50% redesigned, it raised the top speed from 400 mph to 600 mph (640 to 960 kmh). However, the new jet could easily surpass its critical Mach number and crash. For high speed, a different airframe would be needed.

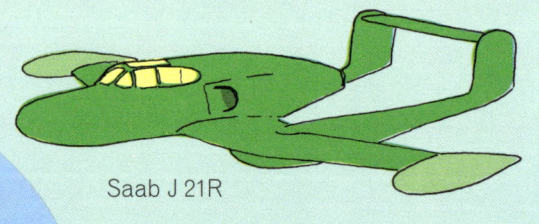
Saab J 21R

Saab began work on the J 29 in late 1945. Since the proposed swept wings were completely new to Saab, they were tested first on a converted light plane. The research paid off, and when the J 29 entered service in 1951 it was one of the best fighters in Europe. It may have been called the "flying barrel," but it was both powerful and well-liked.

Saab J 29

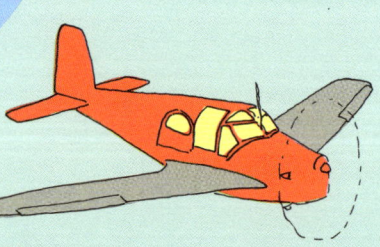
Saab 201 research plane

Even so, Saab was looking ahead to the next generation. The J 32 Lansen also had its wings tested on light planes, and flew brilliantly almost from the beginning. Saab now made planes other Europeans wanted.

But Sweden is a small country with a small market. Saab could design its own planes, but it couldn't spend a lot of time or money doing it. Even one poor product could lead to bankruptcy. Saab had to get it right, every time.

Saab's first project was the Saab 17 bomber. It looks suspiciously like an American dive bomber, and so it should: it was largely designed by American engineers. But they were soon recalled to the States, and Saab was on its own for its next big project, a fighter.

The Saab J 21 was a radical design. Nothing like it had ever been built before. The propeller presented a danger to pilots bailing out, so the J 21 had one of the first ejection seats ever. There were other problems too, but the J 21 became an excellent fighter, and almost equal to the Mustang.

Saab J 32 Lansen

Viggen, Draken and Gripen

The next obvious step was to build a supersonic fighter. So just a year after the J 29 made its first flight, and three years before the Lansen was finished, and in fact only two years after Yeager's breaking of the sound barrier, Saab began studies for a Mach 2 fighter. An additional requirement was the ability to use reinforced roads as runways, since airport runways were vulnerable to attack. By this time Saab had some experience with swept wings and high speeds, but they needed to build an airplane that could fly not only at supersonic speeds, but also at the very slow speeds needed for short takeoff and landing. A new idea was needed.

It was decided to try something completely different: a double delta. The sharply swept inner wings gave the

Saab J 35 Draken

Saab's next fighter was even more innovative: the Saab 37 Viggen (Thunderbolt). It used a delta wing for high speed performance, but had a large canard just above and in front of the wing. This increased not only the lift of the wing, but the maneuverability and short takeoff and landing performance.

Saab 210 research aircraft

high-speed advantages of a delta wing, and the less-swept outer wings gave the advantages of a swept wing, without any of the problems of either type. Moreover, the fat inner wings could easily hold the wheels, fuel, and weapons. But the idea needed testing.

So the Saab 210 was built. It was a 70% scale research airplane with the same 80 and 60 degree swept wings as the proposed J 35 Draken (Dragon). Even with only about ten percent of the power of the Draken, the Saab 210 could fly as fast as 345 mph (552 kmh), and during its 887 test flights proved the double delta concept.

Saab J 35 Draken

But by the time of the Viggen's first flight in 1967, the economic climate had changed in Europe and most countries were holding onto their old fighters longer, or buying cheap American export models. The Viggen was hailed as a brilliant fighter, but few other countries bought it.

In the 1990s Saab built the Saab 39 Gripen (Griffin), which is similar in many ways to the Viggen, but it has had teething troubles, and because it was born after the end of the Cold War, no longer really has a role.

Saab 37 Viggen

The full-scale Draken first flew in 1955, and more than 600 were built before production stopped in 1970. Even then, secondhand Drakens were selling well around Europe.

Instead, Saab has turned to its other lines, the turboprop passenger planes and cars. Saab built its first car for the Swedish market in 1947, partly because the market was there and partly to keep factories busy; today Saab sells hundreds of thousands of luxury cars every year, all around the world. Saab is still, after all these years, getting it right.

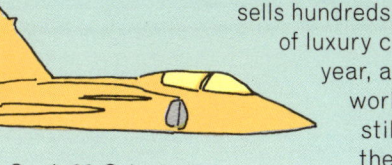
Saab's first car, 1947

Saab 39 Gripen

The Arrow Conspiracies

In the early 1950s the Cold War was beginning to warm up. The United States and its allies were fighting communists in Korea, and the Soviet Union was drawing the iron curtain across Europe. Canadians began to look at the world from a new angle, one with the North Pole in the middle, and realized that any attack on the U.S. by the Soviets would run right over Canada. Some way was needed to defend the huge Canadian north.

American jet fighters didn't have the range or endurance to fly long patrols over the vast arctic tundra. Canada had a fighter of its own, the Avro CF-100, but its straight-wing design was already obsolete. What Canada needed was a new jet fighter that could fly farther, higher, and faster than any other plane in the world.

The Royal Canadian Air Force (R.C.A.F.) asked for proposals from American and British companies, but none wanted to guarantee the performance required. So the R.C.A.F. turned to Avro Canada, who began work on a new delta wing design capable of Mach 2 or more. Almost immediately the team hit a barrier.

There were no wind tunnels fast enough to simulate Mach 2 flight. The solution proved simple, though. Models were mounted on rockets and fired out over Lake Ontario, until a stable design was found.

Development of the Arrow was becoming expensive, and the company had to begin designing a new engine as well as the airframe. So when a new Canadian government was elected, the Arrow program began to look like a good place to cut expenses. Avro Canada had to show Canadians something for their money. On 4 October 1957 the Arrow was officially rolled out in a grand ceremony sure to capture headlines across the country. But this was also the day that the Soviet Union launched Sputnik, the world's first artificial satellite. The coming of the space age, the age of intercontinental missiles, stole the Arrow's headlines.

With the political legs kicked out from under the Arrow, Avro Canada became frantic. They had to show how good their plane was, and fast. In order to get the first five planes into the air as quickly as possible, Pratt and Whitney engines were substituted for the more powerful but still unfinished Avro Iroquois jets. And on 25 March 1958, test pilot Jan Zurakowski lifted the Arrow off the runway at Toronto's Malton Airport for the first of many stunning test flights.

The Arrow's Destruction

There was no prototype Arrow. From the very first (RL 201) built, every plane was a production plane. But even with the first five flying and thirty-two more under construction, the government began thinking about terminating the program and buying American missiles instead. Some say there was pressure from the U.S. to drop the Arrow, partly because they wanted a monopoly on jet fighters, partly because they wanted to sell off surplus missiles, and partly because they resented Canada having better jets than they did. Whether this is true or not, Canada's Ministry of Defense decided the age of manned fighters was over, and began a smear campaign against Avro Canada. The Arrow's true performance (said to be Mach 2.5 or more) was kept secret, and the cost of the fighters was exaggerated, even though it was really less than buying American fighters.

But most of all, Prime Minister John Diefenbaker harbored a deep personal hatred for Avro Canada's flamboyant president Crawford Gordon. Gordon was a protege of one of Diefenbaker's greatest political rivals, and Avro Canada was the third largest employer in Canada, a major political force in itself. The Arrow had to go! So with little warning, on 20 February 1959, "Black Friday," Diefenbaker announced to the House of Commons that the Arrow program was terminated. Gordon retaliated by firing all of his 14,000 workers on the spot, hoping to pressure the government to back down. But Diefenbaker called his bluff, and upped the ante; everything was to be destroyed. Planes, tools, plans, photos, models, drawings...everything. Diefenbaker wanted it to have never even existed. The planes were cut up and sold for scrap, and there would be no recollection of the Arrow now if workers had not taken bits and pieces home with them. What really killed the Arrow? Some people say it was an unexceptional, unneeded airplane, but it feels better to believe it was the victim of a huge international scandal...

There is a legend that one of the Arrows escaped the cutting torch, and was flown off somewhere to be secretly stored until the day comes when it will be needed again. It might not exist, but many Canadians like to think their one and only chance for a great jet fighter is still out there, hidden in a very large barn somewhere, waiting to be found and given the respect it deserved but never really got.

What do you think?

Century Series

After the transsonic F-84 Thunderjet, F-86 Sabre, and F-94 Starfire, came the world's first operational supersonic fighter, the North American Super Sabre. Under the Air Force's numbering system it was the F-100, and it began a series of extraordinary supersonic jet fighters called the Century Series. The Super Sabre entered service in 1954, but some of the series are still in use around the world today.

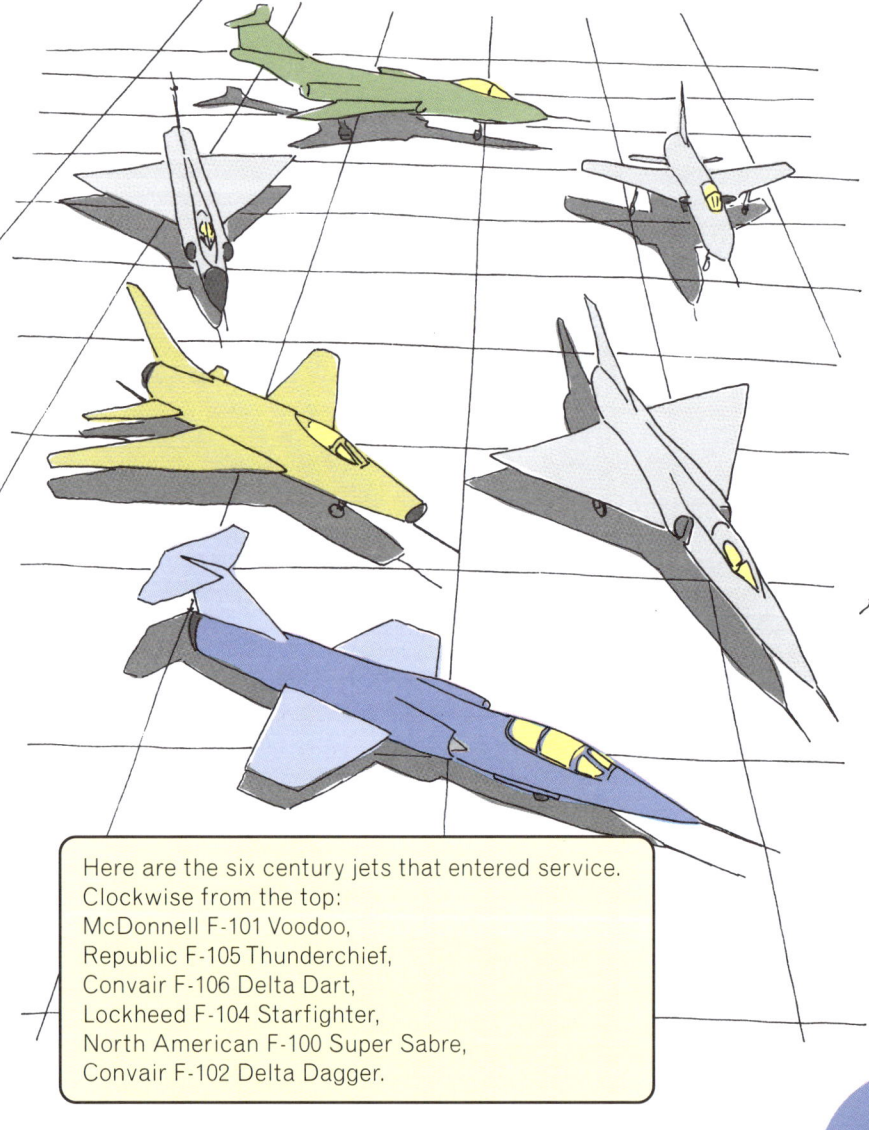

The Convair F-102 Delta Dagger is probably best known now as an example of area ruling, and what happens if it isn't used. Convair had almost finished the prototype Delta Dagger (shown here) when area ruling was introduced, and tried to push their cigar-shaped fighter on the U.S. Air Force (U.S.A.F). But the U.S.A.F. told Corvair supersonic or nothing, and the F-102 got its famous coke-bottle fuselage.

The North American F-100 Super Sabre was the U.S. Air Force's first truly supersonic fighter. Once its initial bad habits had been worked out, it became a favorite of the pilots, and one of the mounts of the Thunderbirds aerobatic team.

Here are the six century jets that entered service. Clockwise from the top:
McDonnell F-101 Voodoo,
Republic F-105 Thunderchief,
Convair F-106 Delta Dart,
Lockheed F-104 Starfighter,
North American F-100 Super Sabre,
Convair F-102 Delta Dagger.

The McDonnell F-101 Voodoo began life as the XF-88, which very nearly went into production but was brushed aside by improved Sabres. Thinner, more sharply swept wings and engines with three times the power turned the Voodoo into one of the most versatile and widely used jets of the century series.

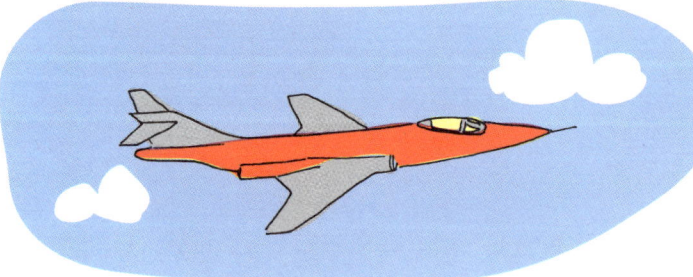

Sleek New Designs

Lockheed's chief designer Kelly Johnson took a fresh approach to supersonic flight. Instead of using highly swept or delta wings, he built tiny straight wings so thin that their edges could cut careless ground crew. The F-104 Starfighter looked more like a missile than an airplane, but it could top Mach 2 almost effortlessly, and was the first airplane ever to hold the world speed and altitude records at the same time. Above are YF-104 development aircraft, still without the distinctive intake cones.

Republic's chief designer Alexander Kartveli liked sleek airplanes, and he thought that area ruling would make his F-105 look like a bowling pin. The original design couldn't be made any thinner, and he didn't want to add bulges to the front and middle. But when he saw the wind tunnel tests, he realized he could have either a sleek airplane, or a supersonic one.

Although there was an YF-107 (below), it never became an F-107. North American began with a Super Sabre and added more power and a dorsal inlet. But at high angles of attack, such as during landing and takeoff, the nose blocked the inlet and starved the engine of air. And so at the end of the 1950s, the Century Series ended with the F-106.

What happened to the other numbers?
F-103: Mach 3 delta by Republic, never built. F-108: Mach 3 delta by North American, cancelled. F-109: VTOL design by Bell, ended at design study stage. F-110: became the McDonnell F-4 Phantom II and began a new series.

The Convair F-106 (above) started out as a modification of the F-102, but almost everything was redesigned and the Delta Dart became a new and much more powerful plane. In December 1959 an F-106 took the world absolute speed record with a 1,525.6 mph (2,440 kmh) flight, and held it for two years. This is the two-seat trainer version.

X-Planes

In the early days of jet development, there was really no way of studying high-speed flight other than actually building a plane and flying it at high speed. Just as in the earliest days of flight, all kinds of peculiar airplanes were built in the name of research. Here are a few.

The Douglas X-3 looks fast from any angle, but it wasn't. The powerful engine it was to have used turned out to be to big to fit, so it didn't have enough thrust to go supersonic except in a steep dive.

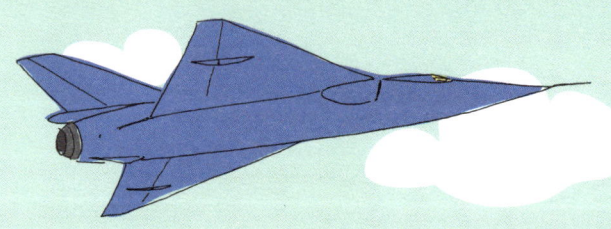

The Fairey Delta 2 was the first aircraft that could take off under its own power to exceed 1,000 mph (1,600 kmh), and set the world absolute air speed record for Britain in March 1956, the last time Britain held it. The Delta 2 was later fitted with new wings and a droop nose to do research for the Mach 2 Concorde.

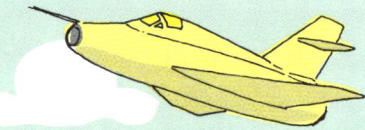

France's SFECMAS Gerfaut was the first european airplane to exceed the speed of sound in level flight, which it did on 3 August 1954. It could reach Mach 1.3, largely because the bulgy fuselage made good use of area ruling. (This plane was one inspiration for the Kingfisher model in this book.)

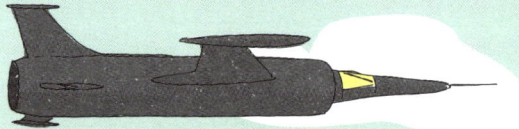

France's Leduc 022 was undeniably one of the ugliest airplanes ever built. The pilot sat in an ejectable pod in front of a huge ramjet engine, and was launched from the back of a cargo plane to make transonic flights and land on skids.

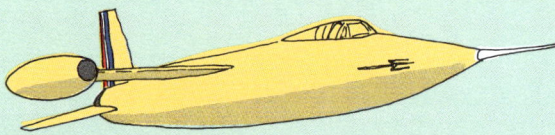

For a time mixed power airplanes were in vogue, and France's Sud Ouest 9000 Trident was one. As the name implies, it had three engines: two wingtip jets for cruising and a rocket motor in the back for high-speed combat. It could reach Mach 1.6, but only for four and a half minutes.

For many years the U.S. Air Force thought the main role for fighters was bomber escort, but the early jets had such short ranges this was impossible. The McDonnell XF-85 Goblin was designed as a parasite fighter, carried with folded wings inside a B-36 and launched from a trapeze when needed. But returning to the trapeze proved almost impossible, and the program ended after several crashes.

Germany's Messerschmitt P.1101 (top) was almost ready for test flying at the end of the war, and was brought back to the States for study. It was designed with wings that could change their amount of sweep, from 35 to 45 degrees, to counteract aerodynamic changes that occur near the speed of sound. The Americans built the Bell X-5, with wings that could swing from 20 to 60 degrees, to test the idea. It worked well, and was later used on many operational fighters.

The Handley-Page H.P.115 was built to test the slow-speed characteristics of wings with extreme sweep. It puttered along at several hundred mph, with several different types of leading edge fitted.

Exotic Jets

By the 1980s, supersonic wind tunnels and computer modelling had replaced trial-and-error in designing supersonic fighter jets. But experimental planes were still needed, not to test new ways of going fast, but to test ways of maneuvering and fighting once up to speed. Here are a few interesting experiments.

One way to make a jet extremely maneuverable is to change the direction of the jet stream. Vectored thrust works like the outboard motor on a boat, swinging the tail. The X-31A uses vectored thrust to perform maneuvers that would be impossible for a conventional fighter. The F-22 Raptor now uses this technology.

Advances in materials have made exotic planes possible. The Junkers Ju 287 had trouble with its forward-swept wings because aerodynamic forces threatened to tear its metal wings off. The extremely stiff wings of the X-29, made of a composite material much like an exotic fiberglass, could withstand much more flexing, and so testing of the maneuverability of swept-forward wings began again. The X-29 was controlled by a computer; it is so unstable no pilot could fly it unaided.

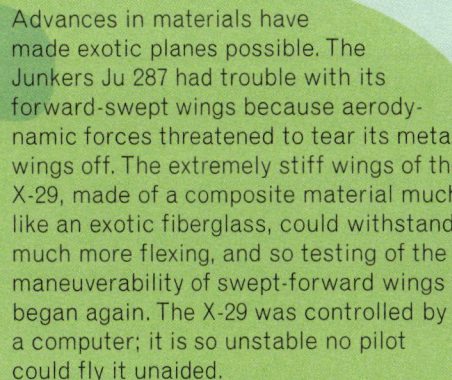

The McDonnell-Douglas X-36 sports something that looks like a cockpit, but it is really a small, unmanned technology demonstrator. What it demonstrates is the ability of thrust vectoring to control an airplane without a vertical tail, a configuration that would be completely unflyable otherwise. A jet's rudder shows up clearly on radar, and getting rid of it would increase the plane's stealthiness. This plane is very new, and rudderless fighters are still in the future.

Boeing's X-32 was built as one of two competitors in the Joint Strike Fighter fly-off. The winner was Lockheed-Martin's X-35, which will be developed into a fighter for use by the Air Force, Navy, Marines, and several other services abroad. The requirement was for one basic airframe that could be flown conventionally, from an aircraft carrier, and even vertically. The X-32 proved to be excellent at all three roles, but would have had to be redesigned with a stabilizer.

Vertical Jets

Airplanes are restricted in their usefulness by having to take off and land at airports. We all find it frustrating to have drive way out to an airport on the outskirts of the city when we take a trip, but for fighters the airport is even more of an Achilles' Heel. If the runway is unusable, so are the fighters. So for many years designers have been experimenting with VTOL airplanes, airplanes that take off and land vertically. And the power of the jet engine has made it possible. But the road to success has been rocky...

Rolls-Royce saw commercial applications in VTOL very early. To test the concept, in 1953 they built the "Thrust Measuring Rig", which is universally known as the "Flying Bedstead." Two lift engines pointed down, and puffer jets on outriggers provided control.

France's SNECMA C.450 Coleoptere looked promising, if bizarre. Tests with the pilot sitting atop a jet engine with puffer jet controls proved that controlled hovers were possible. Even with the annular wing added hovering went fine. But the ring-shaped wing proved more dangerous than expected, and the plane crashed during a transition from vertical to horizontal flight. The pilot bailed out of the aircraft, and France bailed out of the development program. To me, this plane has always looked like a person in a barrel of very hot water. Did the designer feel the same?

One of the earliest VTOL projects was planned by Focke-Wulf during World War II, but never built. It had ramjets at the end of three rotor-like wings, which would have spun at high speed and allowed the plane to fly both vertically and horizontally.

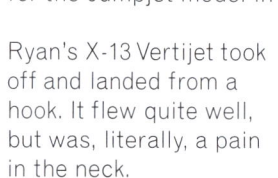

Germany's EWR Sud VJ 101C had four engines in wingtip pods that could swivel down and be joined by another two lift engines in the fuselage for vertical flight, which were dead weight in level flight. This was one inspiration for the Jumpjet model in this book.

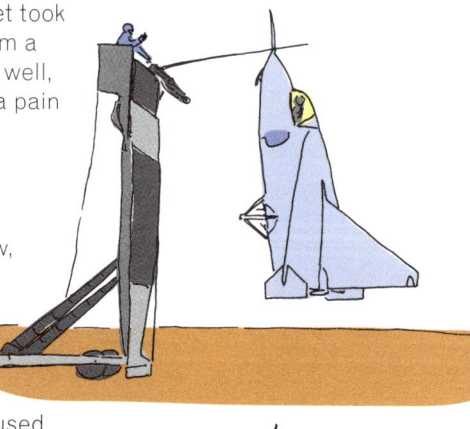

Ryan's X-13 Vertijet took off and landed from a hook. It flew quite well, but was, literally, a pain in the neck.

At the same time Avro Canada was building the Arrow, another division was building the Avrocar, a flying saucer ordered by the U.S. Air Force. It used three jet engines to spin a lift fan in the center for hovering, and excess exhaust was vented out the sides to push it along. It was meant to fly supersonically at high altitude, but only ever managed 30 mph (48 kmh) at a height of one yard (roughly one meter).

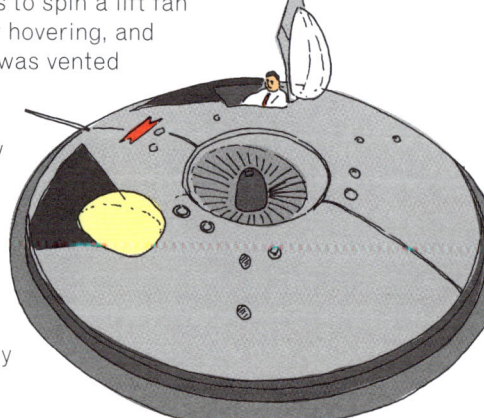

The Hawker Harrier

Hawker's revolutionary P.1127 research aircraft made its first free hovering flight on 19 November 1960. It was made possible by an equally revolutionary engine from Bristol Siddley, the Pegasus. The Pegasus has a large fan in front that blows air both into the engine itself, and out through adjustable nozzles in the front. The jet exhausts through similar nozzles at the back, and all four can be swivelled back for level flight or down for vertical takeoffs and landings.

The P.1127 was developed into the Hawker Harrier, still in service in the U.S. and Britain. It makes up for not being supersonic by its extreme versatility and its ability to land almost anywhere. This was demonstrated on 5 May 1969 by Sdn. Ldr. Tom Lecky-Thompson of the RAF, when he nearly won a *Daily Mail* prize for the fastest trip from the top of the London Post Office to the top of the Empire State Building. The flight portion began from a coalyard at St. Pancras Station, and 6 hours 11 minutes later the Harrier was in New York. The winner flew supersonically, but lost time travelling to and from airports.

One of the latest VTOL projects is Lockheed-Martin's X-35. This will be developed into the Joint Strike Fighter. The X-35 will be supersonic, be stealthy, and for the Marines, be able to take off and land vertically. The Marines now fly Harriers, and while these have been updated regularly, they are still a thirty-five year-old design. When the X-35 pilot pushes a lever forward, doors open on the top and bottom of the fuselage, and a lift fan driven by a shaft from the engine starts to lift the front half of the plane. At the same time, the exhaust vent turns down 90 degrees to lift the back. The fan alone produces about 18,000 pounds (8,180 kg) of thrust, half the power needed to drive an aircraft carrier.

Skunk Works

Be Quick, Be Quiet, Be on Time

As World War II continued, it became clear that fighters could no longer be made better by giving them more power and bigger propellers. Jets were going to be needed to provide the power and speed essential for air superiority. But the first American jet fighter prototype, the Bell XF-59 Airacomet, turned out to be a dud. In 1943 the Army Air Forces asked Lockheed to develop a jet fighter using the British de Havilland Goblin centrifugal flow engine. And Lockheed asked a young engineer named Clarence "Kelly" Johnson to build it. Johnson decided to try something new: he set up a small project team to design and build the plane outside the normal bureaucracy, in a place where engineers and shop artisans could work together without intermediate layers of management. The idea was radical, but Johnson had promised a flying prototype in 150 days, so Lockheed had no choice but to let Johnson do it his way.

Johnson and his engineering school friend Don Palmer began setting up the department and writing the guidelines that would become the Skunk Works' operating rules. Johnson insisted on autonomy, speed, and cooperation, and the rules made the approval of drawings and purchase of materials much faster and easier. There was no room for the team in the Lockheed Burbanks factory, so the team built a shack out of old crates and canvas next to the wind tunnel building and got to work. And on 13 November 1943, 140 days after work began, the XP-80 was finished (above). After a few engine problems were worked out, test flying began, and it was soon clear that the design was a winner. It was scaled up a little to make the XP-80A production prototype, this time taking eighteen days

longer than the promised 120 days. The XP-80R, modified with an afterburner, was also used to set a world speed record in June 1947, flying at 623.8 mph (1,000 kmh); this was the United States' first speed record in a quarter century (above).

After the plane was built and the test flying passed on to the Army Air Forces, Kelly Johnson turned the production of the new fighter over to the usual Lockheed departments, and disbanded his team. This was to become typical of the Skunk Works; it would design and build a prototype quickly, quietly, and on time, and after a little flight testing turn the project over to another group for production. The XP-80A became the P-80 Shooting Star, and more than 1,700 were used in the States and overseas for almost a decade before being replaced.

Spy Planes

The F-104 began when Lockheed sent a proposal for a lightweight fighter to the U.S. Air Force in 1952. The prototype was finished in a year, by a Skunk Works-like team headed by Kelly Johnson. The razor-thin wings stuck out only seven feet on each side, making some pilots wonder if there were any wings at all. But this Mach 2 fighter was a bestseller.

In the mid-1950s the Soviet Union was developing long-range missiles with nuclear warheads, and the CIA found they couldn't rely on the military for information. So they asked Johnson to build a spy plane that could fly so high it would be unstoppable. The result was the U-2, which could fly for hours at 80,000 feet (24,458 m). The Soviets eventually learned how to shoot down the U-2, but forty-five years after its first flight, it is still flying reconnaisance missions today.

The CIA was concerned about its spy planes' survivability, and asked the Skunk Works to study the effect of speed, altitude, and low radar-detectability on the plane's ability to avoid being shot down. Johnson began designing a plane that could fly at more than Mach 3, and when the CIA insisted on reducing the radar signature the A-12 was born. The chines on the side of the fuselage both lowered its visibility to radar and held fuel for long flights. The fuselage and wing were blended and the rudders canted inwards to lower detectability further. The plane had to withstand temperatures of more than 800 degrees from the air friction at Mach 3.2, and the engines had to work at altitudes of up to 90,000 feet (27,515 m), the edge of space. It also pioneered the use of titanium, which required very careful handling. The A-12 first flew in 1962, and although it was one of the most advanced airplanes ever, it was designed with slide rules. The slightly larger SR-71 flew for years, and with none ever being shot down.

How the Skunk Works does what it does

The rules that Kelly Johnson and Don Palmer drew up for Skunk Works operations allow the project team to work independently of the usual company bureaucracy, and therefore build quickly and sucessfully, and maintain the secrecy essential to many of their programs. Engineers work together with designers and shop workers, usually only steps away from each other, to make communication instant and mutual understanding possible. Here is a summary of how the Skunk Works is able to develop prototypes of highly advanced aircraft in very little time and at very low cost.

• Project office teams are small but strong.
• The program manager has complete control, which allows him to meet technical, cost, and schedule objectives.
• The staff is kept as small as possible, and everyone's responsibility is big.
• Communications are continuous and open and focus on joint problem-solving.
• Involvement by outsiders is restricted.
• Requirements are challenging but achievable, and once set are changed as little as possible.
• Schedules are kept tight, but the possibility of delays and setbacks is taken into account.
• Expenditures are tightly controlled and costs are reviewed regularly.
• Contracts are kept free of restrictive or unnecessary provisions.
• Specifications and proposals are limited in size and detail.
• Reports and other paperwork are kept to a minimum.
• The focus is on engineering design, but manufacturing, testing, materiel supply, and logistics support are considered early in the process.
• A simple and flexible engineering drawing system is used to eliminate delays.
• The Skunk Works does the early test flying in order to get direct feedback on its products.
• Security is maintained as tightly as is required by the program.
• As much as possible all personnel work in the same place.

On the other hand, the Skunk Works doesn't produce the aircraft it designs. The regular production facilities are better for doing that, and the Skunk Works team stays free to begin work on its next project.

Stealth Jets

Although the A-12 and SR-71 had a very low radar cross section (RCS), and attempts had been made to make the U-2 less detectable to radar, the Soviets knew exactly when and where they were flying. Even halving the RCS with curves and chines only gave the plane a few extra miles before detection. In order to go undetected, or be detected too late to be stopped, the RCS had to be reduced ten thousand times or more. And this wasn't possible, until Lockheed made a lucky find. In the early 1900s James Maxwell and Arnold Sommerfield developed formulae to predict how geometric shapes would reflect microwave energy. In 1962 the Soviet scientist Piotr Ufimstev used them to determine the radar return of two-dimensional objects. And when Lockheed engineer Denys Overholster came across this paper, he realized that it could be used to make an airplane almost invisible to radar, an airplane that could sneak up on an enemy, attack, and get home before anyone knew it was there. Stealth was born. The basic idea is that carefully angled facets would reflect radar waves away from the radar antenna, so that the radar wouldn't "see" it. The Skunk Works got to work designing the stealthiest airplane possible, and came up with the Hopeless Diamond. To the radar, the 32-foot (9.8 m) model looked the same size as a golf ball, but without wings or a tail the diamond shape had no hope of flying.

The Skunk Works tested the stealthiness of the Hopeless Diamond, Have Blue, and F-117 with models mounted on poles in front of extremely powerful radar. But since the radar was strong enough to detect an ant at a distance of a mile, the pole itself showed up more strongly than the model, and Lockheed had to spend half a million dollars designing a stealthy pole. Then the radar operators couldn't find the model of the Hopeless Diamond. "It must have fallen off the pole," they said, but when a crow landed on the model the operators shouted "Now we have it!" The Have Blue RCS was so small that bird droppings doubled it. The stealth planes weren't invisible to the radar, but they looked so small (more like bumble bees than planes) that they wouldn't be detected until it was too late.

The Hopeless Diamond won a stealth design competition against Northrop, so the next stage was to design an airplane that could actually fly. Lockheed didn't have the computing power to calculate the RCS of curved surfaces, so Skunk Works engineers designed an airplane made entirely of flat planes and sharp corners. The aerodynamicists claimed it would never fly without curves to reduce drag, but wind tunnel tests showed that it could, if it had a tail and wings. The design that emerged was the Have Blue demonstrator (above). Have Blue's wings were swept an extreme 72.5 degrees, and two small rudders were canted inwards. There were no right angles, because right angles reflect radar waves too well, and the engine inlets and exhaust outlets were placed on the top to protect them from being seen from below. Special radar absorbing materials were used on the surface, but much of the airplane was made from ordinary aluminum and bits of other planes. And on 1 December 1977, it took off for its first flight.

The Have Blue demonstrated that stealthy flight was possible, but also showed many problems, most of which were fixed in the F-117 Nighthawk. The production F-117s were built in secret, tested in secret, operated in secret, and until revealed in the early 1990s remained completely unknown. But since then it has

become a symbol of power and high technology. It is painted black to look menacing; although black is the most easily seen color in any light, and a light pastel colour would be much better, real pilots don't fly pink airplanes...

I've never seen a picture of the Hopeless Diamond, but my guess is that it looks something like this. Lockheed claims it couldn't be made to fly, but I have flown paper airplanes shaped like this. And I know they look very small to radar, because when I flew one at dusk a bat mistook it for a bug and tried to eat it...

Drastic Design Changes

The YF-22, which the Skunk Works designed in competition with the Northrop YF-23, had to be both stealthy and supersonic. Incredibly, Lockheed still didn't know how to calculate the RCS of curved surfaces, so the Skunk Works engineers gave up trying to use a computer to design it and just put hundreds of clay models into the radar range. This kind of trial-and-error design hadn't been done since the 1950s, but it paid off. The YF-22 was almost as stealthy as the F-117, and could not only fly past the speed of sound but cruise there without using the afterburner, one of the first airplanes ever that could. The production F-22 Raptor is now being readied for operational use.

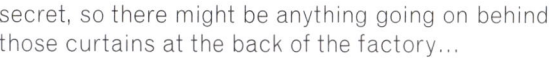

won't be another new jet fighter program in the U.S. for maybe twenty years. By that time, even the Skunk Works may have forgotten how to build one. Then again, the Skunk Works operates largely in a hidden world, in absolute secret, so there might be anything going on behind those curtains at the back of the factory...

But even before the F-22 is sent to squadrons it may be replaced by the JSF, the joint strike fighter planned for use by every air arm in the United States and Britain. One design used by all would save time and money in maintenance, and a huge production run would reduce the cost of each plane. It has to be stealthy and be able to cruise supersonically and have a VTOL version as well. This was the holy grail of fighter contracts, and the Skunk Works won it with their two X-35 demonstrators.

Jet fighter design has changed drastically from the early days, when a prototype could be built and flown in half a year. The latest designs take as long as a decade to go from concept to production, and may cost tens of billions of dollars. The Skunk Works approach to aircraft design makes this process faster and cheaper. But even so, modern fighters are expected to have longer operational lives, and there probably

Jets on Display

There are many retired fighter jets on display in aviation museums around the world. Here are a few of the jets you can build and fly with this book.

a The Lockheed T-33 was a trainer developed from the P-80 Shooting Star. This one is on display at the R.C.A.F. Memorial Museum in Trenton, Ontario, Canada.

b The Musee de l'Air et de l'Espace in Paris houses many unique French jets. And out on the tarmac is this Swedish one, a Saab Draken, looking ready to go.

c Trenton's F-86 Sabre is a Canadian version that was used by the R.C.A.F. Golden Hawks aerobatic display team.

d This is the MiG-15 in the Royal Air Force Museum in Hendon, England.

e Trenton's F-5 looks fast even when it's standing still.

f The CF-104 in the Canadian Warplane Heritage Museum in Hamilton, Ontario is a Canadian-built version of the F-104 Starfighter.

g This is all that's left of the Arrow, the nose of the sixth plane built. It is carefully preserved in the National Aviation Museum in Ottawa.

h This Grumman X-29 was retired to the ceiling of the Smithsonian's National Air and Space Museum in Washington.

Author's father in a Meteor

Assembling the Avro Arrow

Building and Flying Fifteen Paper Jets

The following + marks indicate the difficulty of the plane; + is fairly easy, and +++ will take some work. Carefully read the instructions before cutting and gluing, and start with some of the easier ones first.

Jumpjet sheet 1 +
There are many ways to build jet fighters that can take off and land vertically, and therefore do without airports or aircraft carriers, and most of them have been tried over the years. This model is based on a German experimental plane with jet engines on its wingtips, which swivelled 90 degrees downwards for vertical flight. The original barely flew, but the Jumpjet will fly quite high, and rarely lands vertically.

Hornet sheet 2 +
The Hornet is based on the F/A-18 Hornet, whose distinctive twin rudders sprout from the fuselage between the wing and the stabilizer, instead of the very back as is usual. They are so big and effective that they produce more dihedral effect than is needed. I had trouble flying the prototype until I reduced the stability by turning the wings down instead of up. And suddenly it flew like... well, like a jet.

Kingfisher sheet 3 +
For many years the only way to learn about supersonic flight was to actually get in a test plane and fly past the sound barrier, because wind tunnels couldn't simulate supersonic speeds. Experimental jets were built one after the other, and either flew or didn't. The Kingfisher is a mixture of bits from several early French designs. The hunched shoulders, long nose, and swept back wings suggested the name.

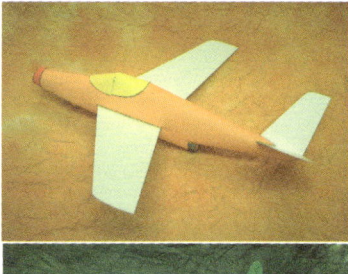

Vulcan sheet 4 ++
There is a jet bomber called the Vulcan, one of the stars of the Falklands War (along with the Harrier jump jet), but this plane just borrows its name from the same place: the Roman god of fire. The design itself was inspired by some of the secret German fighter jet projects that surfaced after World War II. Its V-tail makes adjusting a little different than usual, but the Vulcan is easy to fly, if you have lots of room.

Lockheed P-80 Shooting Star sheet 5 ++
The Shooting Star was the first jet fighter to reach production in the United States. It was intended for the Pacific War, but although it was designed and built in an unbelievable 150 days, it wasn't ready in time for action. With an extra yard of fuselage and another seat it became the T-33 trainer, still in use today. The air intakes on the model look like they should create a lot of drag, but I think you'll find they don't.

Messerschmitt Me 262 sheet 6 ++
This was the first operational fighter jet in the world, but it nearly didn't get off the ground. The very first prototype was flown with a propeller in front instead of jet engines. The next version had a tailwheel, and could only get its tail up if the pilot pumped the brake hard at high speed and hoped it didn't nose over. But at last, with a nosewheel, it became one of the most effective fighters of the war...just too late.

North American F-86 Sabre sheet 7 ++
The Sabre started its life as a straight-winged fighter, not much different from any other of its day. But the straight wing created too much drag at high speeds to be either effective or safe. When U.S. scientists got their hands on German research data and captured Me 262s, they realized the answer to their problem was the swept wing. With new wings, one of the greatest airplanes of all time streaked into history.

Scimitar sheet 8 +
When I designed this plane I had the MiG 15 and MiG 17 in mind. But they have their wings in the middle of the fuselage and their stabilizers in the middle of the rudder, which make them difficult to build. The Scimitar turned out to be easy to put together and easy to fly.

Northrop B-49 sheet 9-10 ++
The B-49 isn't strictly a fighter, but the pilots who flew it said it performed like one. Jack Northrop had always believed that all-wing planes were the wave of the future. He based several small flying wing planes on an experimental German all-wing fighter, the Horten Ho IX, and then built the propeller-driven B-35. By the time this was flying the jet age had arrived, and it was converted to the eight-engined B-49. But neither entered service, and it wasn't until the B-2 that Northrop's dream came true.

Avro CF-105 Arrow sheet 11 ++
There is a legend that when the Arrows were being destroyed, one managed to escape the cutting torch and is hidden in a barn somewhere, waiting perhaps for a day when it will be needed again. I preferred not to wait, and built my own version.

Saab Draken sheet 12 ++
This is a model that nearly didn't happen. The first time I flew it, in a schoolyard, it went over the fence and I spent half an hour trying to find it. So I went to a bigger park, and this time it flew about two hundred meters and landed right in front of a moving bicycle... More than eight years later I worked up the courage to try again. And here it is (although I did lose one prototype on a roof).

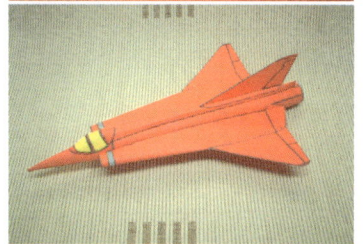

Lockheed F-104 Starfighter sheet 13 +++
When Lockheed's test pilot Tony LeVier first saw the Starfighter, he asked "Where are the wings?" To be sure, the "missile with a man in it" looks more like a rocket than an airplane. I chuckled when I first saw LeVier's remark, but I laughed out loud when my editor looked at the plans for this plane and said, "Where are the wings?"

Northrop F-5 Tiger sheet 14 +++
In the 1960s, as jet fighters were getting bigger and heavier, Northrop decided what the world needed was a small, lightweight fighter, one which would have the same performance as the big fighters on a fraction of the power and at a fraction of the cost. The result was the F-5, which was a bestseller around the world for thirty years. You may wish you had a third hand when you build this model, but it is worth it.

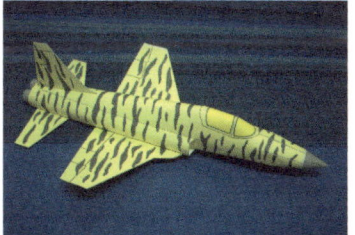

Grumman X-29 sheet 15 +++
The X-29 was built to test whether swept-forward wings really could give good performance at both high and low speeds. But the quest for extreme performance and handling led to a shape that was essentially unstable. If the onboard computer ever malfunctioned, the X-29 would be out of control in a couple of seconds. The basic lack of stability made this model something of a challenge...

Lockheed F-117 Nighthawk sheet 16 +
The F-117 is another unstable airplane. On top of the extreme sweepback in the wings, which tends to make the plane want to flip onto its back at low speeds, there are no curved surfaces to help reduce drag. But this model will fly well as long as the speed doesn't drop. The secret is in the forward location of the center of gravity and the upturn of the nose; the plane sort of surfs on the air.

Tools

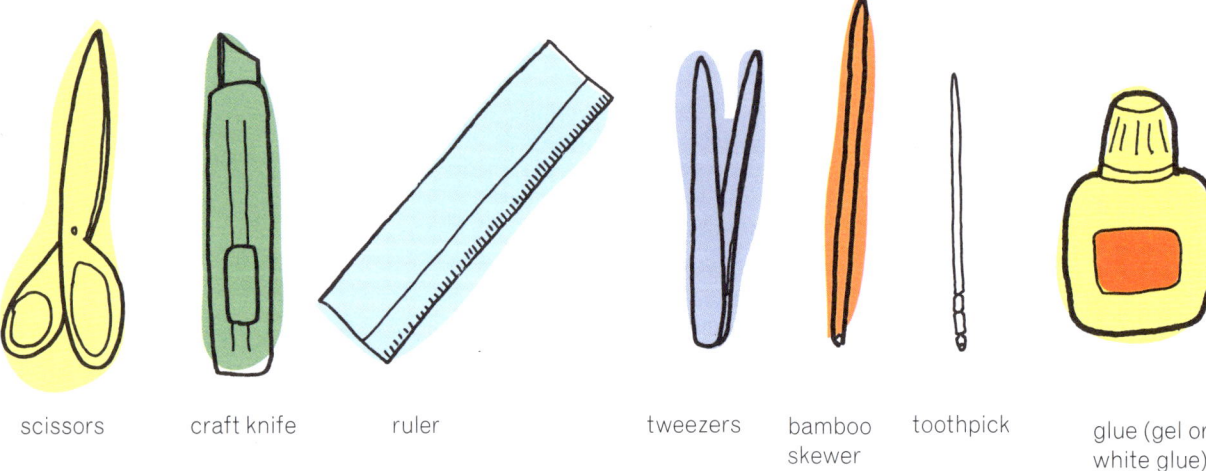

scissors craft knife ruler tweezers bamboo skewer toothpick glue (gel or white glue)

Folding

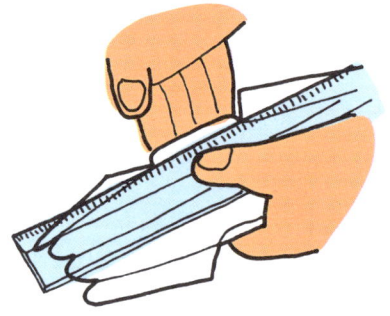

Use a ruler to make crisp and accurate folds. This is especially important when folding narrow parts.

These are the types of lines used in the kit pages. Be sure not to fold on the alignment lines!

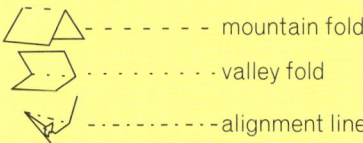

mountain fold
valley fold
alignment line

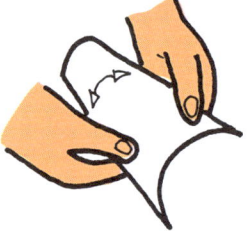

Bend curved parts into shape carefully, a bit at a time, with your fingers. Too sharp a bend will crease the paper.

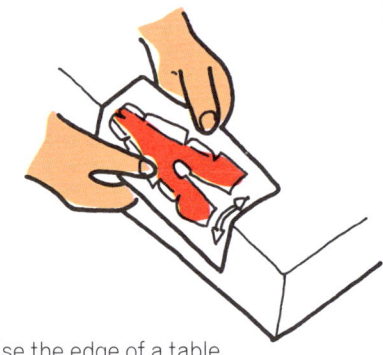

Use the edge of a table to "train" a curve into the paper.

The camber, or curve, in the wing is what creates the lift that holds the plane up. Add camber by gradually bending the wing as shown. In the case of swept wings, just bend the leading edge down slightly.

straight wing   front ———— back
swept wing   front ———— back

Cutting

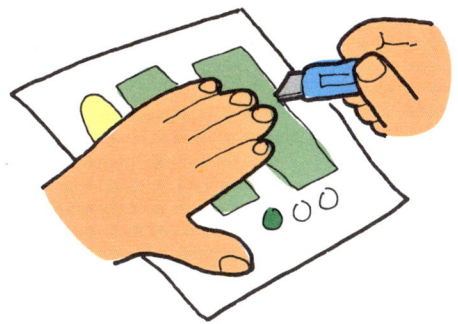

You can push out the larger pieces with your fingers, but the paper will be less likely to bend or tear if you use a craft knife to cut them loose. Cut out the small parts carefully with scissors.

Carefully trim the flash from around the edges of parts you have pushed out. This will make them look cleaner and fit together better.

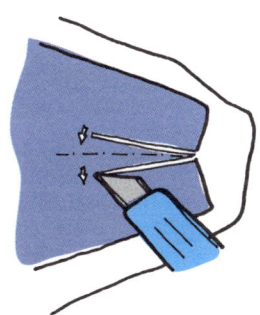

Make little cuts at the ends of slits for wings and tails before you cut out the part. Don't cut out the whole slit until you have bent and glued the fuselage together, or the paper will fold instead of curve. When you are ready to glue the tail or wing in place, hold the fuselage gently as shown and cut the slit gradually, in several light passes.

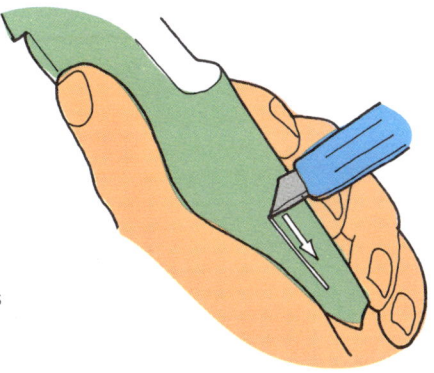

Don't worry if you accidentally cut the wrong thing. In most cases you can patch up the cut from the inside with a small tab of paper. Butt the two cut edges together and glue the patch behind it, or between two parts. If the patch is small, it won't affect the balance of the airplane.

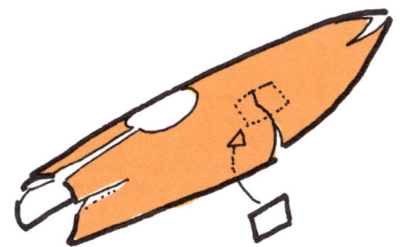

Gluing

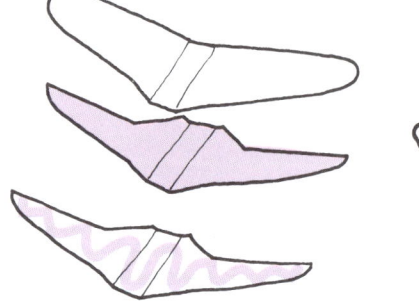

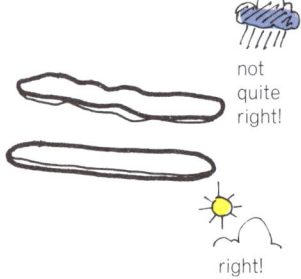

Spread glue evenly over the whole of surfaces to be glued together. Just a bead of glue will not be strong enough to hold the plane together in flight!

If you are using a water-based glue, like white glue, spread it as thinly as possible when gluing together wing parts, or the water in the glue will warp the finished wing.

You can use a toothpick to spread glue evenly over the paper.

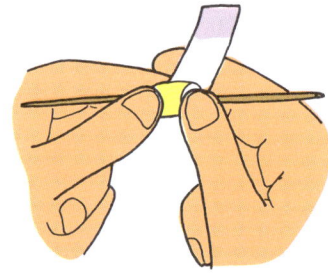

Ballast parts are rolled tightly around a skewer or toothpick. Glue only the last half inch of each long strip, and the first half inch of each strip after that. When the last strip is glued in place, pull out the skewer and square up the end of the ballast roll.

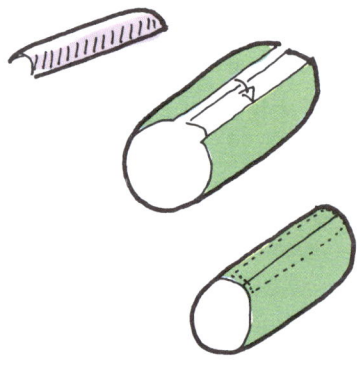

Cylindrical parts use a separate glue flap, which is glued in place half at a time. After the first half is firmly set, spread glue on the remaining portion, and close the cylinder with the edges butting together.

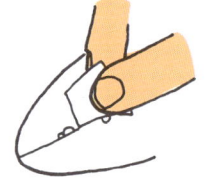

The finished plane will look much nicer if you wipe away excess glue. A scrap of paper works well.

Make glue fillets by applying a bead of glue to the seam and spreading it with your finger or a tissue.

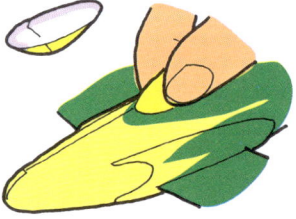

For parts without glue tabs, put a thin bead of glue around the inside edge, and hold them in place gently until the glue grips.

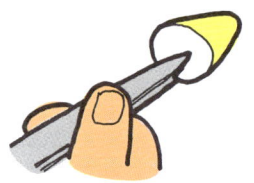

For smallish parts, use tweezers to press the glue flaps firmly in place.

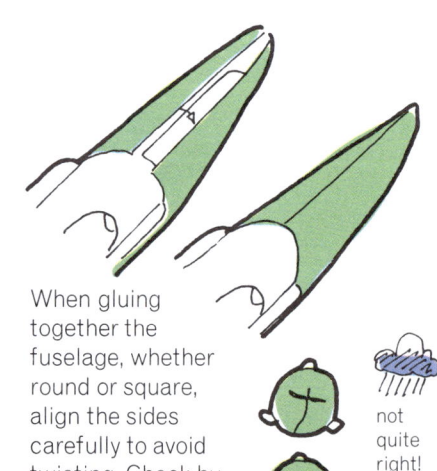

When gluing together the fuselage, whether round or square, align the sides carefully to avoid twisting. Check by looking at the part from behind. If it is twisted, carefully pry apart the seam and reglue it.

Test Flying

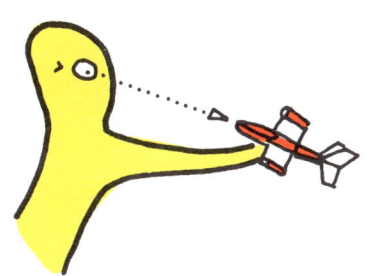
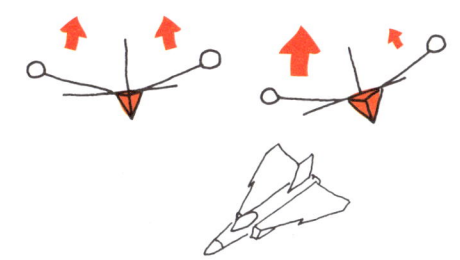

The upturn of the wings is called dihedral. It helps keep the plane level, because when the plane banks the lift created by the lower wing increases, and straightens the whole plane to where the lift is equal again. But the large angle of sweep in delta wings has the same effect, so they need no dihedral.

Your plane won't fly well if the wings are warped or twisted. You can check alignment by holding the model at arm's length and examining it from the front and back.

Fix warps by gently twisting the wings and tail with your fingers.

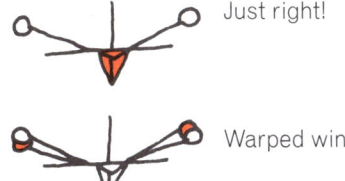

Just right!

Warped wings!

Warped tail!

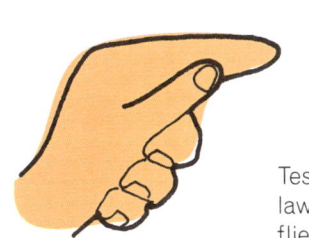
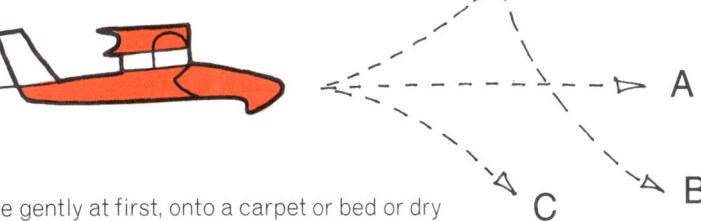

Test fly the airplane gently at first, onto a carpet or bed or dry lawn. Toss the plane firmly straight forward and watch how it flies. If it stalls or dives, adjust it and test fly again, until it glides gently like pattern A.

A

Just right!

B

Fix a stall by bending the rear of the stabilizer down slightly.

C

Fix a dive by bending the rear of the stabilizer up slightly.

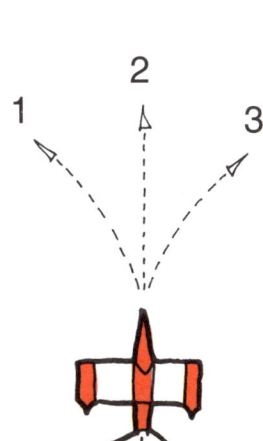

If the plane turns to one side or the other, adjust it until it flies straight as in pattern 2.

1

Fix a left turn by slightly bending the rear edge of the left wing down, the rear edge of the right wing up, and the rudder right.

2
Just right!

3
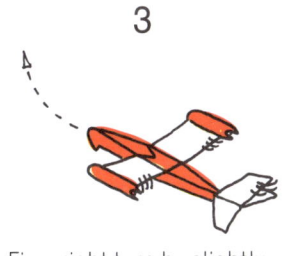
Fix a right turn by slightly bending the rear edge of the left wing up, the rear edge of the right wing down, and the rudder left.

Outdoor Flying

Fly Safely

Paper airplanes fly much faster than one expects, and they can be dangerous to eyes. Always fly away from trees, power lines and roads, and never point the plane towards people or pets.

Most of the planes in this book can be flown outdoors, and if thrown properly will stay in the air quite a long time. Choose a large grassy field for flying, and always launch from the upwind end of it. For the safety of the plane, you should avoid wet grass and strong or gusty winds.

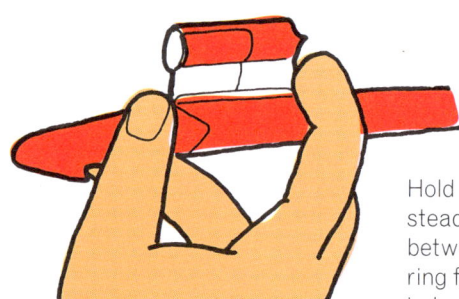

Hold the plane like this, steadying the fuselage between the thumb and ring fingers, and with the index and middle fingers behind the wings. Tilt the plane away from you and slightly upwards.

Throw the plane the way you would a ball, complete with follow through, but without spinning it. Throw the plane lightly several times to get the hang of it before putting all your strength into it.

Using a Catapult

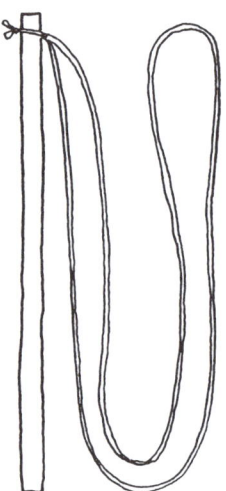

Here's the catapult...

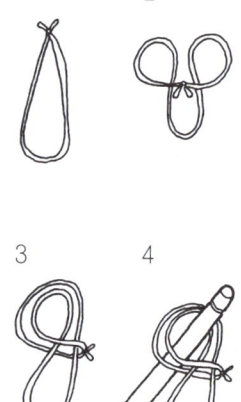

...and here's how to make it, using model airplane rubber and a stick or pencil.

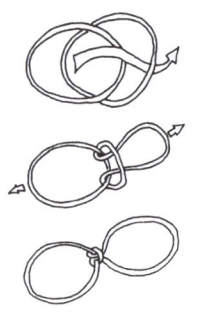

You can also string together two or three rubber bands instead of the rubber thread.

Launch the plane 45 degrees or more from the horizontal, and at between 45 and 90 degrees of bank. If the plane loops straight into the ground, change the hands you hold the plane and catapult with.

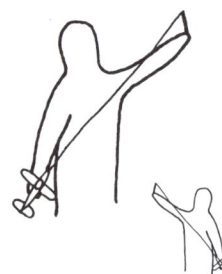

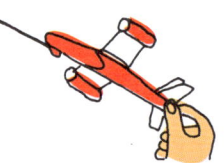

Hold the plane gently by the very back of the fuselage.

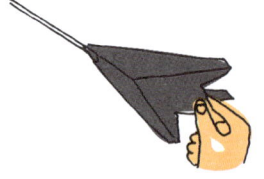

Some planes, like the F-117 and the X-29, have to be held by the back of the wing or the rudder. Be careful not to twist it while launching.

Flying Tips

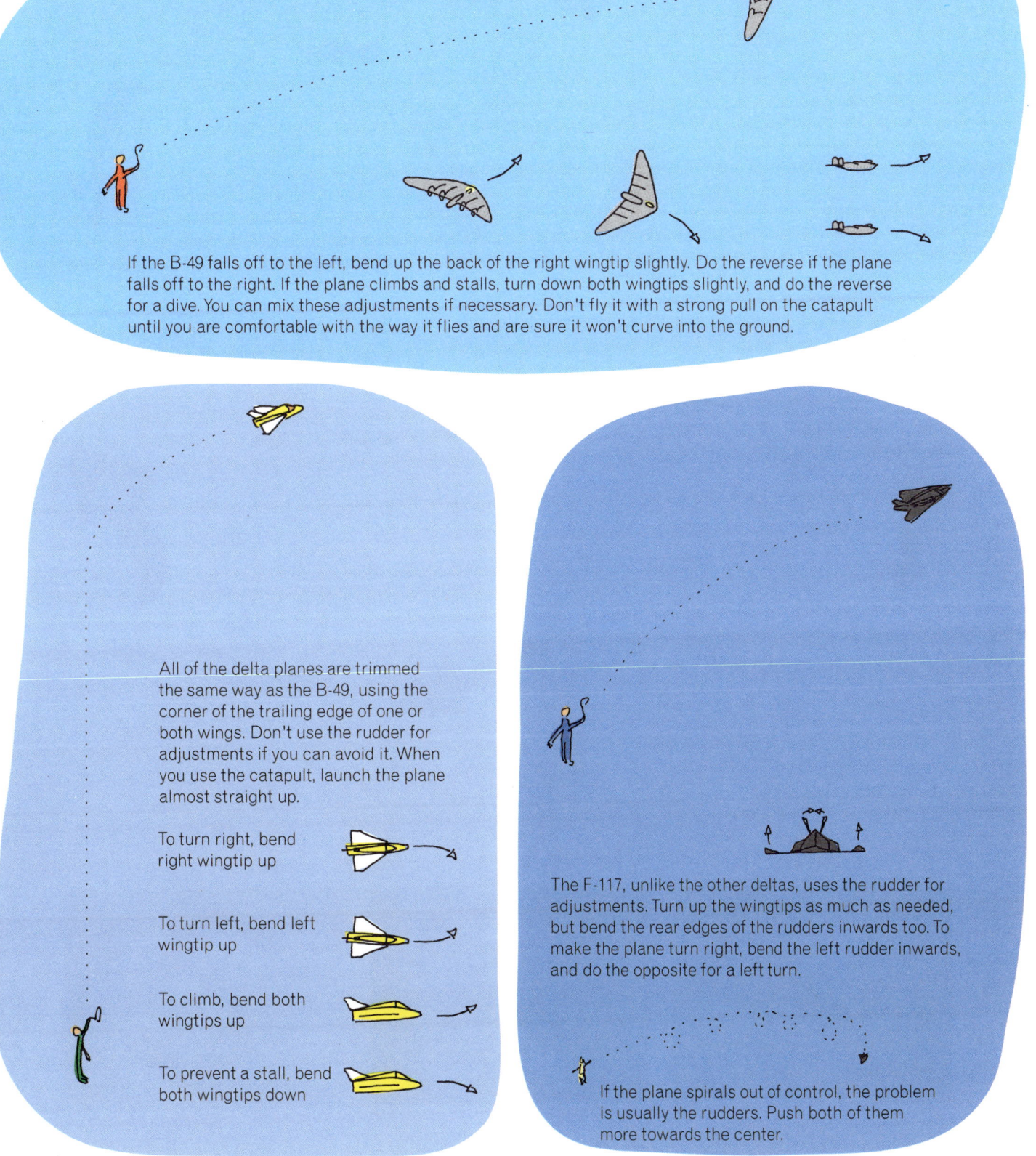

If the B-49 falls off to the left, bend up the back of the right wingtip slightly. Do the reverse if the plane falls off to the right. If the plane climbs and stalls, turn down both wingtips slightly, and do the reverse for a dive. You can mix these adjustments if necessary. Don't fly it with a strong pull on the catapult until you are comfortable with the way it flies and are sure it won't curve into the ground.

All of the delta planes are trimmed the same way as the B-49, using the corner of the trailing edge of one or both wings. Don't use the rudder for adjustments if you can avoid it. When you use the catapult, launch the plane almost straight up.

To turn right, bend right wingtip up

To turn left, bend left wingtip up

To climb, bend both wingtips up

To prevent a stall, bend both wingtips down

The F-117, unlike the other deltas, uses the rudder for adjustments. Turn up the wingtips as much as needed, but bend the rear edges of the rudders inwards too. To make the plane turn right, bend the left rudder inwards, and do the opposite for a left turn.

If the plane spirals out of control, the problem is usually the rudders. Push both of them more towards the center.

For all of the planes, launch them lightly with the catapult once or twice to see which way they tend to turn. If the plane tends to curve to the right, hold it with your left hand and use the catapult with your right. Do the opposite for planes that curve left.

Jumpjet sheet 1

Fold the tips of wing 1, gently bend the curved engine portion, and fasten the glue tabs on the bottom of the wing to make two tubes as shown. (photos A and B)

Bend wing reinforcement 2 as shown, and glue it to the bottom of the wing, flush with the leading edge. (photo C)

Fold and glue parts 2 and 3 to make the rudder.

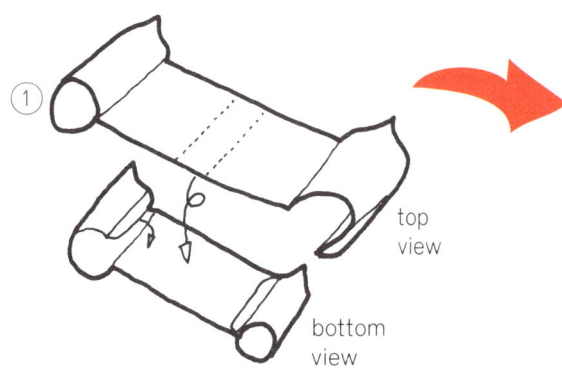

top view

bottom view

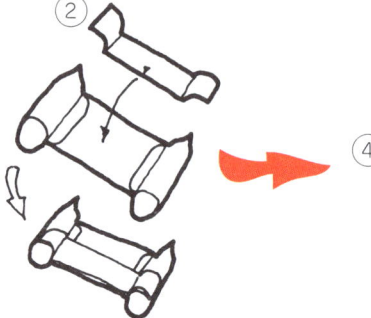

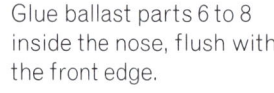

Fold fuselage 5 as shown, but make only a light crease along the centerline. Glue the front flaps inside the nose. (photo D)

Glue ballast parts 6 to 8 inside the nose, flush with the front edge.

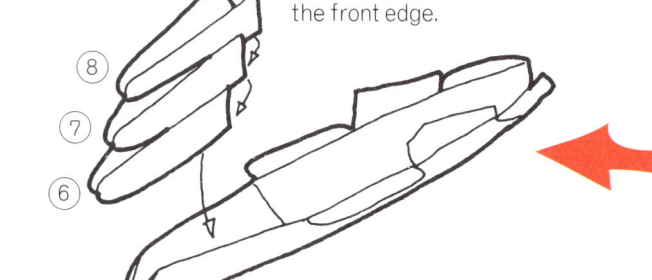

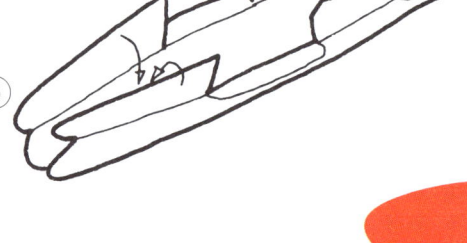

Glue the flaps at the top of the fuselage.

Apply glue to the inside of nose 9 and slide it onto the front of the fuselage until it butts against the wing glue tabs. The hooks should meet at the bottom. (photo E)

A Gently curve the wingtips with your fingers. A round pencil or knitting needle might also help.

B Align the two folds when you glue the wingtips, so the engine tubes will be straight.

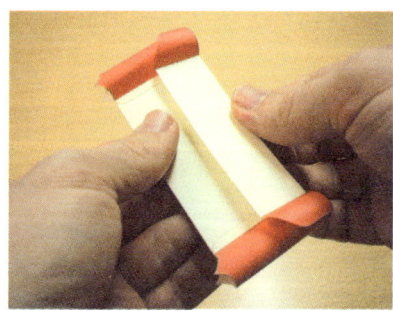

C Bend the wing reinforcement into shape before gluing it to the bottom of the wing.

Glue the back of the fuselage together.

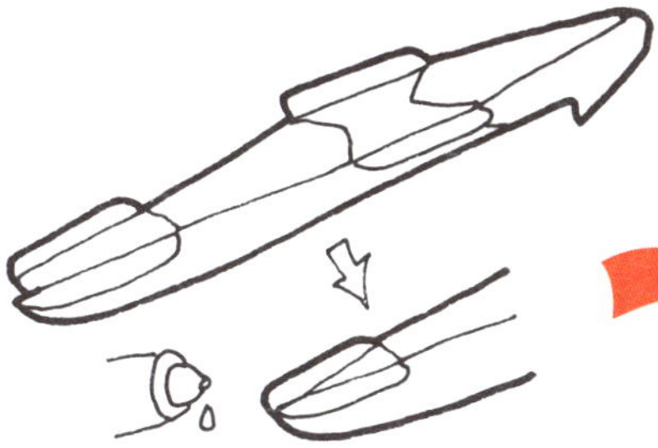

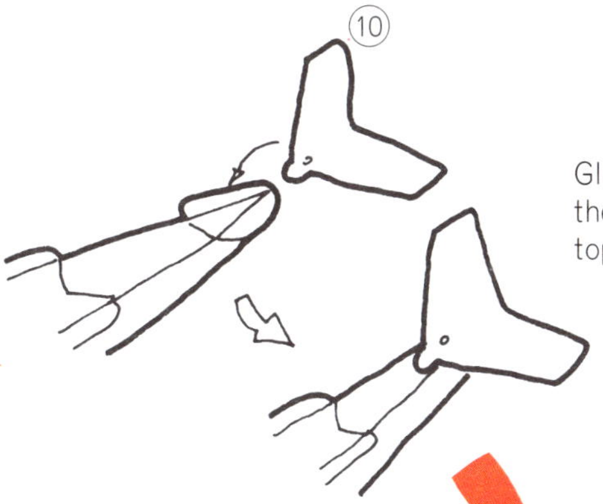

Glue the stabilizer 10 to the rear glue tabs and the top of the fuselage.

Line up the rudder with the dot on the stabilizer and glue it in place.

Glue the wing to the fuselage as shown. The front slips under part 9 but over the tab at the back. (photo F)

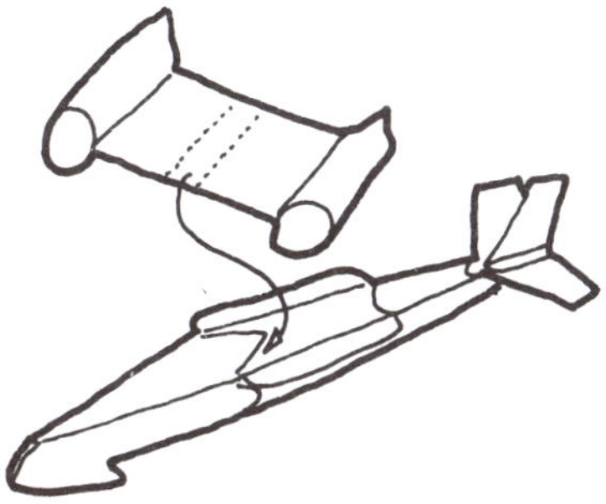

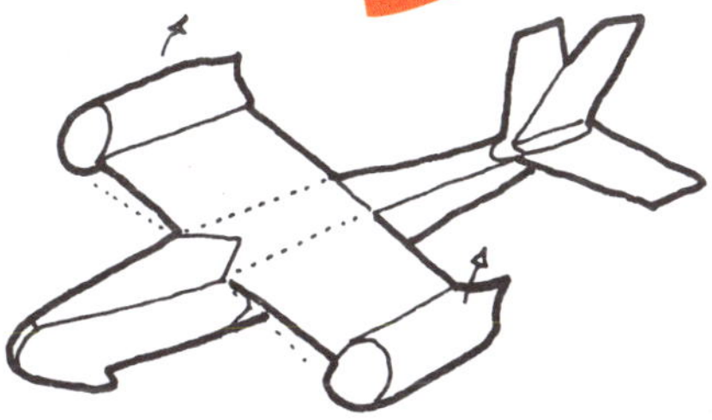

Fold the wings slightly where they meet the fusealge to give about 10 degrees of dihedral.

D Glue the two front flaps inside the fuselage.

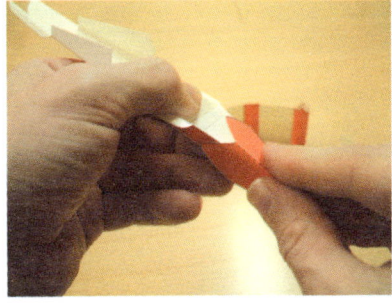

E The nose part slides on neatly if you hold it as shown. Keep the fuselage open and steady with your other thumb.

F Glue the wing under the tab on part 9 as well as to the fuselage glue tabs.

Hornet sheet 2

Fold and bend the fuselage into shape as shown. Glue the front flaps inside the nose.

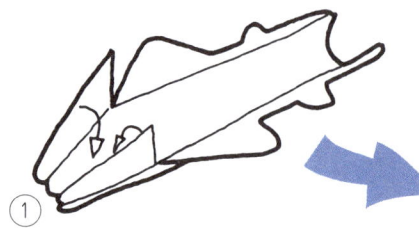

Glue the two ballast parts 2 and 3 inside the nose, flush with the front edge.

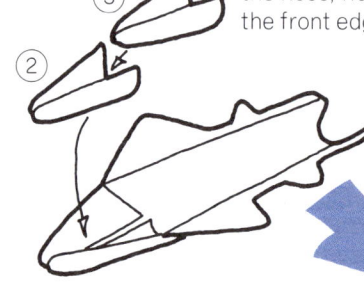

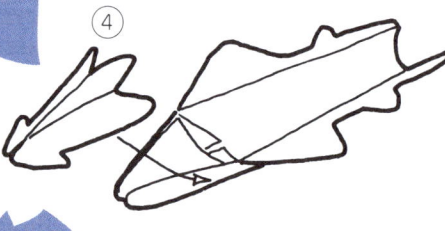

Apply glue to the inside of nose part 4, and slide it onto the nose to glue it in place. It should butt against the wing glue tabs, and the hook should meet at the bottom.

Glue wing 5 under the flap on part 4 and all along the fuselage glue tabs. Make sure the rear corners of the fuselage meet the marks on the wing.

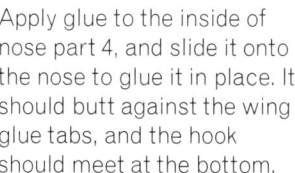

The completed nose will look like this.

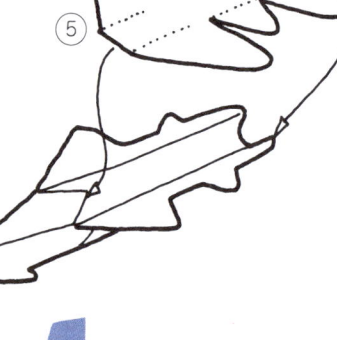

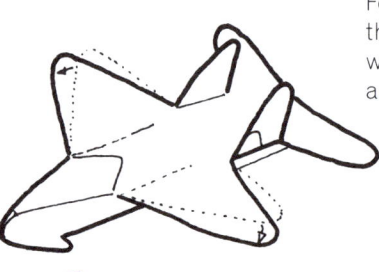

Fold the wings down where they meet the fuselage, to give wings from 5 to 10 degrees of anhedral (minus dihedral).

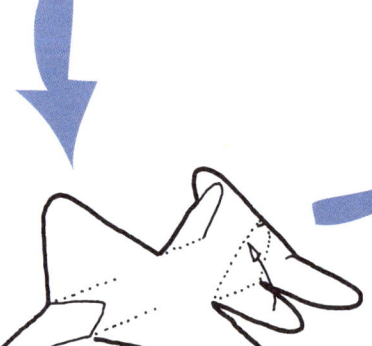

Fold the two rudders up until they are almost vertical.

From the side it will look like this...

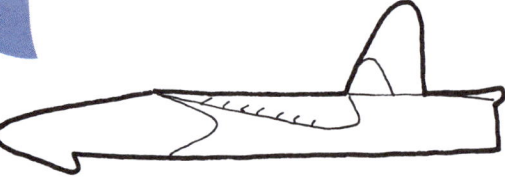

Bend down the leading edges of the wings to give them camber as shown.

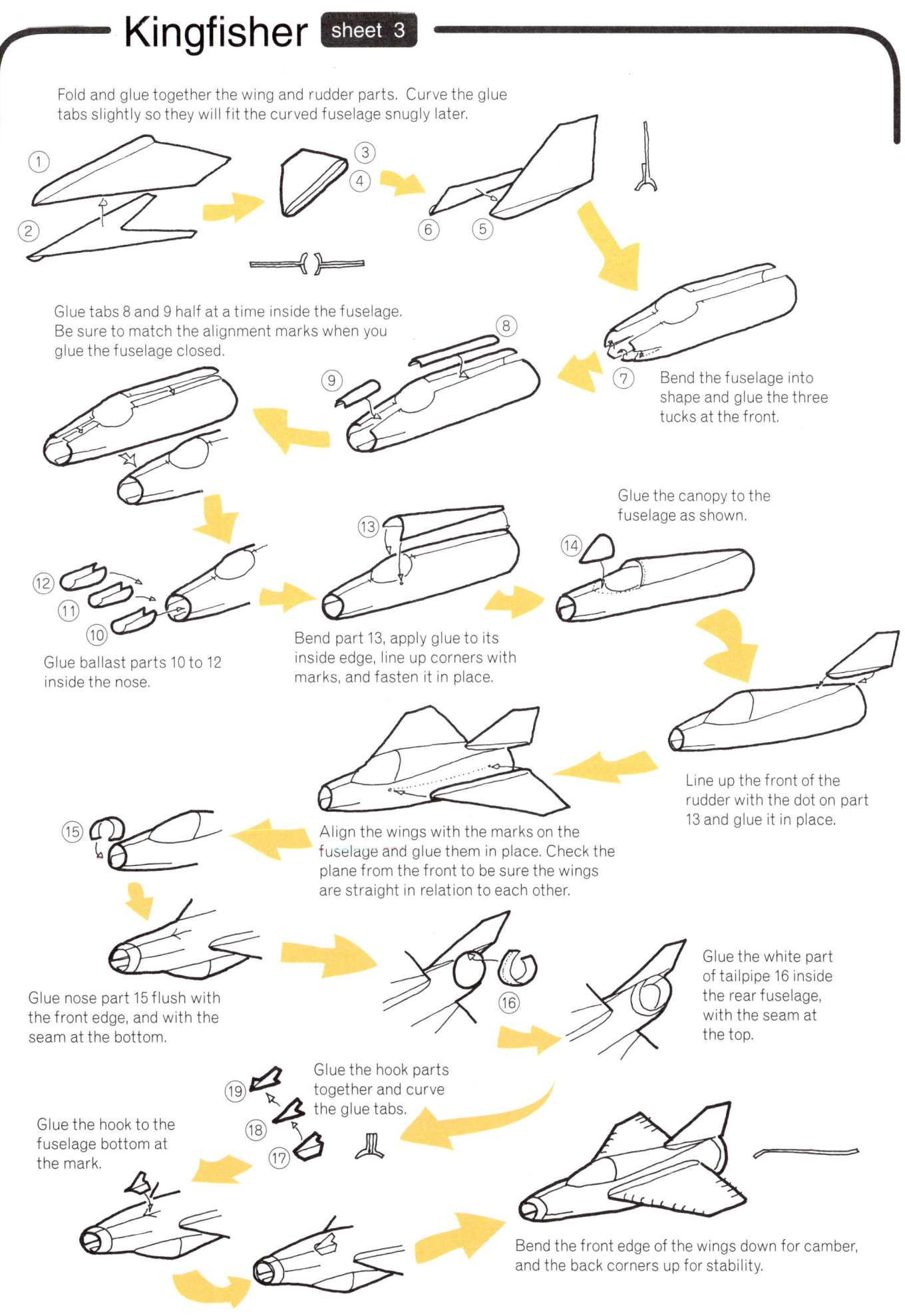

Vulcan sheet 4

Fold about 10 degrees of dihedral into wing parts 1 and 2, and glue them together.

Fold about 35 degrees of dihedral into tail parts 3 and 4, and glue them together.

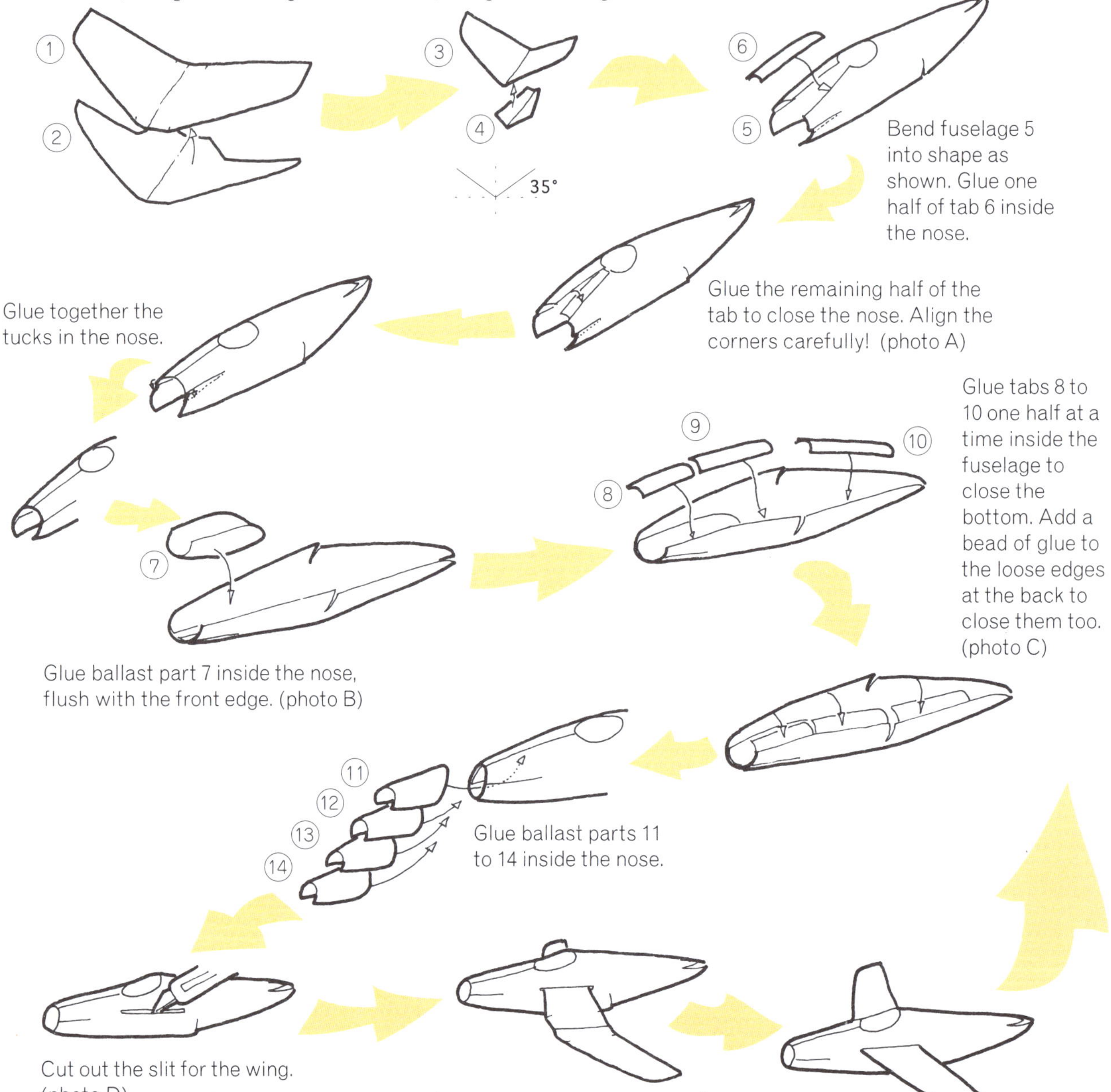

Bend fuselage 5 into shape as shown. Glue one half of tab 6 inside the nose.

Glue the remaining half of the tab to close the nose. Align the corners carefully! (photo A)

Glue together the tucks in the nose.

Glue ballast part 7 inside the nose, flush with the front edge. (photo B)

Glue tabs 8 to 10 one half at a time inside the fuselage to close the bottom. Add a bead of glue to the loose edges at the back to close them too. (photo C)

Glue ballast parts 11 to 14 inside the nose.

Cut out the slit for the wing. (photo D)

Slide the wing in place, and after using the alignment marks to center it, fix it in place with light beads of glue along each seam. (photo E)

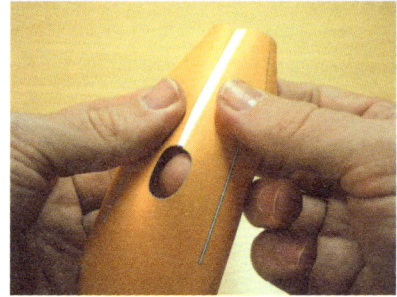

A Curve the fuselage and tab before you glue them. The edges butt together and meet at the corners.

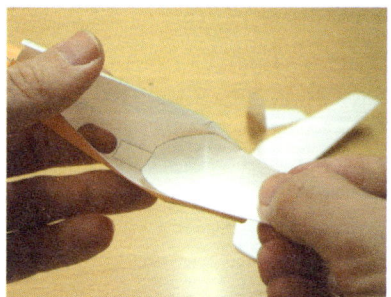

B Glue ballast part 7 inside the nose before you close the bottom of the fuselage.

C It is easier to glue part 10 in place before parts 8 and 9. Seal the loose edge at the back with a little seam of glue.

Slide the tail into the slit at the back of the fuselage. After checking from the front and back to make sure it is straight, fix it in place with light beads of glue.

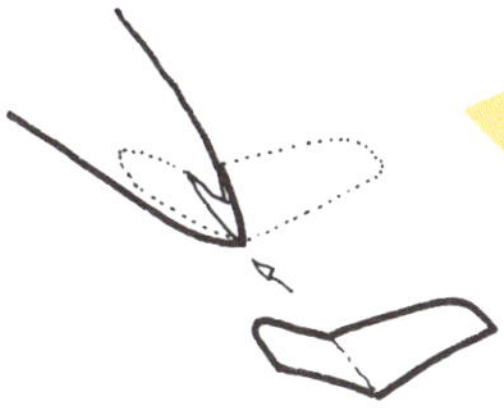

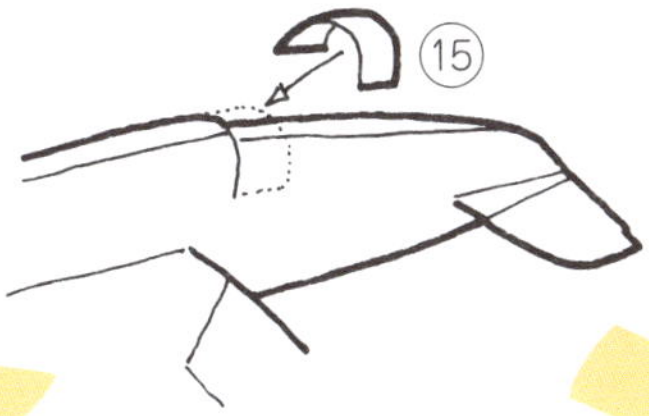

Glue tailpipe 15 to the inside of the opening in the bottom and to the side of the fuselage.

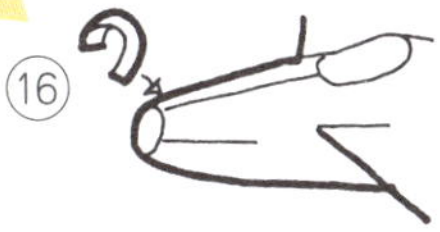

Glue part 16 over the nose, flush with the front edge and with the seam at the bottom.

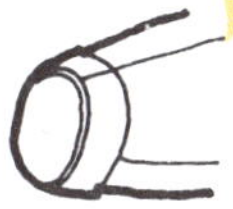

Glue the tucks in part 17 to make the canopy.

Apply glue to the inside of the canopy and glue it in place on the fuselage. (photo F)

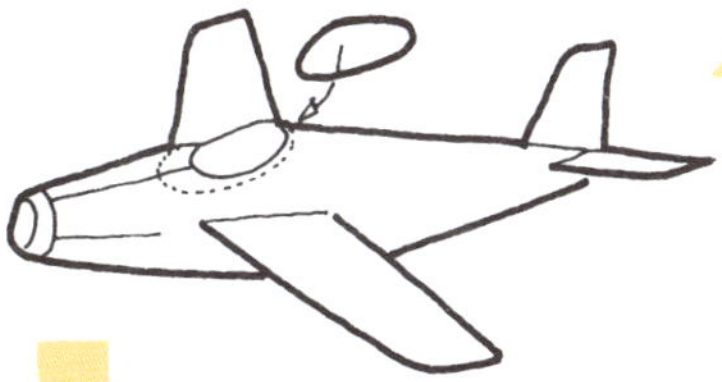

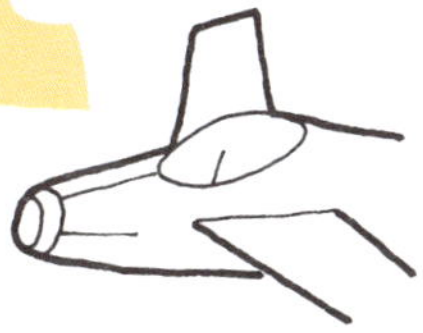

Glue the hook parts together.

Glue the hook to the bottom of the fuselage at the mark.

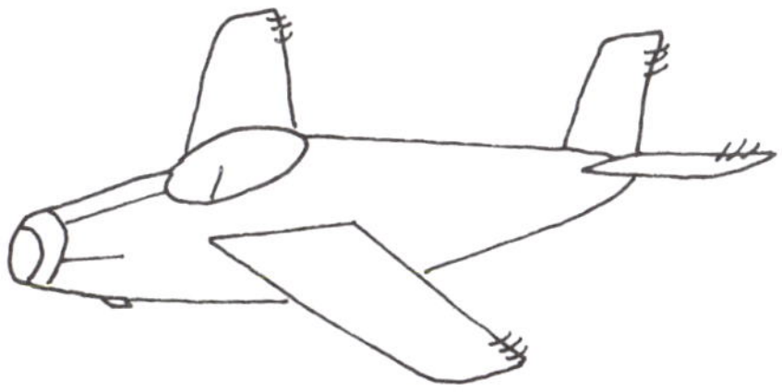

After adding camber to the wings, turn up their outside back corners slightly, and twist up the trailing edges of the tail a small amount.

D Cradle the fuselage gently while cutting the slit. Make the cut in several light passes.

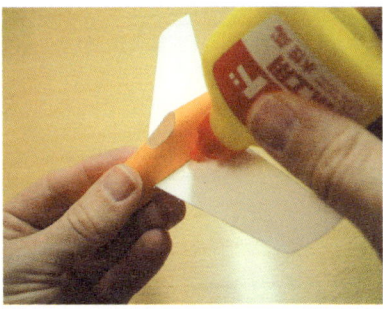

E Fix the wing in place with light beads of glue. A dot of glue spread with a toothpick or your finger gives the best result.

F Apply glue to the inside edge of the canopy. Press it in place and hold it lightly until the glue firms enough to keep it in place.

47

Lockheed P-80 Shooting Star sheet 5

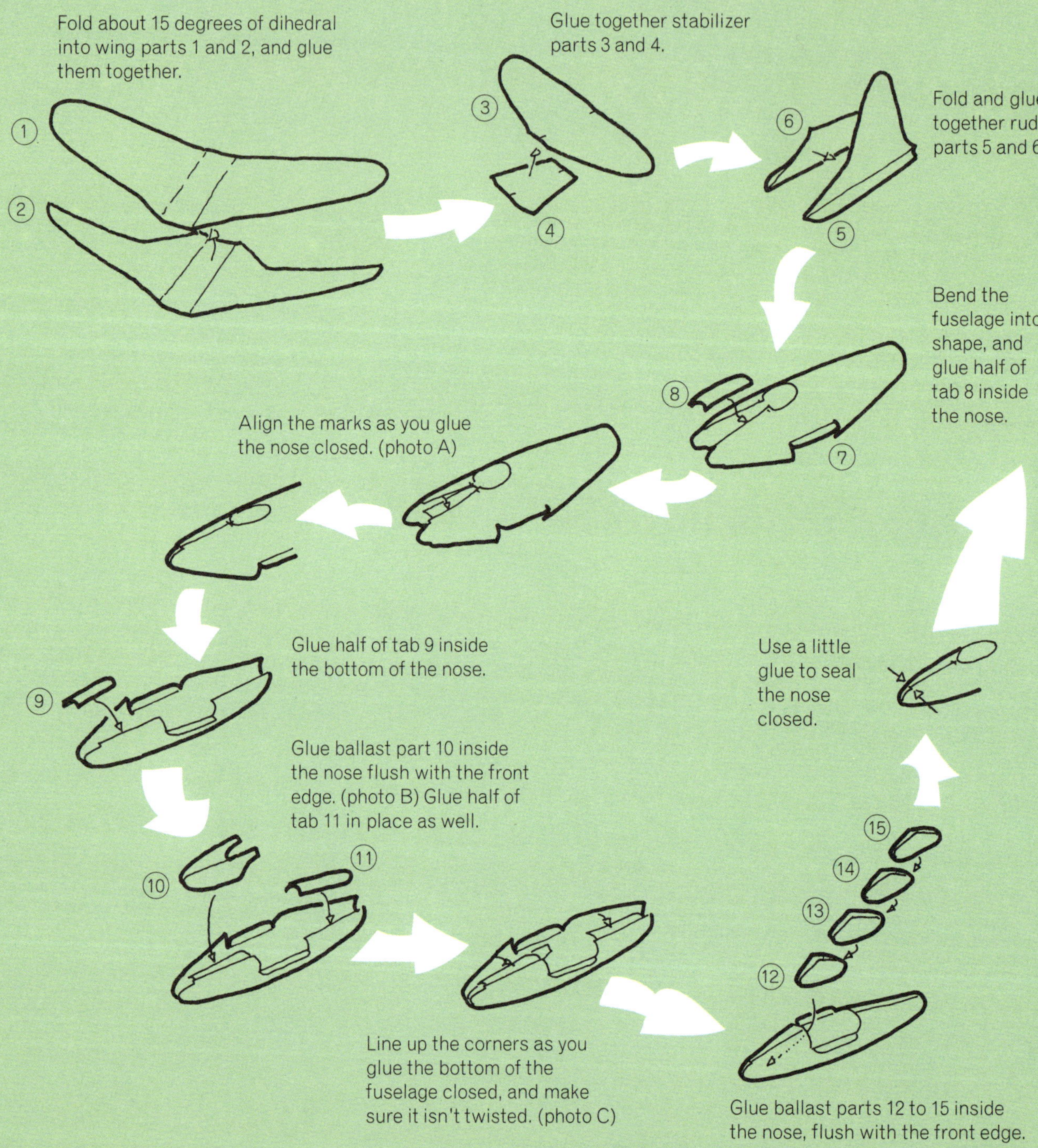

Fold about 15 degrees of dihedral into wing parts 1 and 2, and glue them together.
1
2
Glue together stabilizer parts 3 and 4.
3
4
Fold and glue together rudder parts 5 and 6.
6
5
Bend the fuselage into shape, and glue half of tab 8 inside the nose.
8
7
Align the marks as you glue the nose closed. (photo A)
Glue half of tab 9 inside the bottom of the nose.
9
Glue ballast part 10 inside the nose flush with the front edge. (photo B) Glue half of tab 11 in place as well.
10
11
Line up the corners as you glue the bottom of the fuselage closed, and make sure it isn't twisted. (photo C)
12
13
14
15
Glue ballast parts 12 to 15 inside the nose, flush with the front edge.
Use a little glue to seal the nose closed.

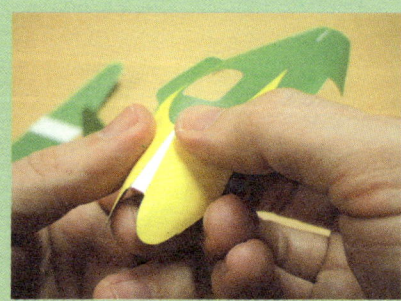

A Align the edges of the nose carefully as you glue them together, but work quickly.

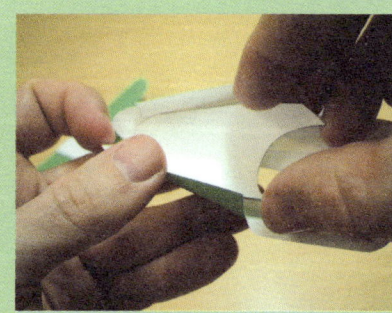

B Glue ballast part 10 in place before you close the bottom of the fuselage.

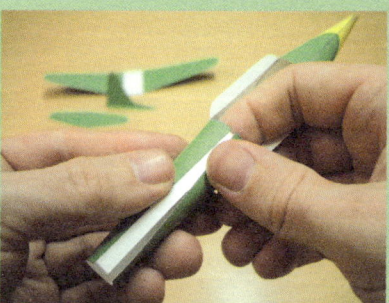

C If you curve the fuselage and tab parts before you glue them, they will fit together more snugly.

Carefully cut out th slits for the stabilizer. (photo D)

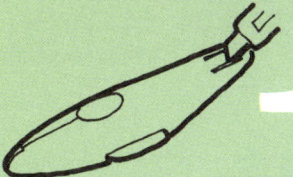

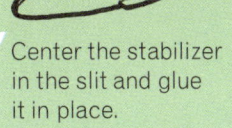

Center the stabilizer in the slit and glue it in place.

Align the rudder with the dot on the fuselage and glue it in place.

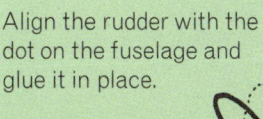

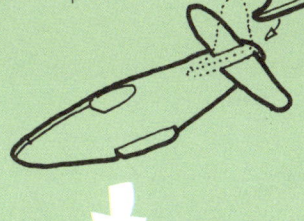

Glue the wing firmly in place. Check from the front and back that the fuselage isn't twisted.

Bend inlets 17 and 18 into shape and cut out the slits. Put glue around the inside edge, slide them over the wing, and glue them in place with the front corners over the dots on the fuselage. (photo F)

Apply glue to the inside edge of part 16 and glue it to the wing and the bottom of the fuselage. (photo E)

Glue the tucks in part 19 to make the canopy.

Apply glue to the inside edge of the canopy and attach it to the fuselage as shown.

Glue the hook parts together.

Glue the hook to the bottom of the fuselage at the mark, add camber to the wings, and you're done!

D Cut the slits for the stabilizer.

E Bend part 16 into shape before gluing. Hold it with your fingers until the glue hardens a little.

F Line up the front corners of the inlets with the dots on the fuselage when you glue them.

Messerschmitt Me 262 sheet 6

Bend (not fold) about 15 degrees of dihedral into wing parts 1 and 2, and glue them together.

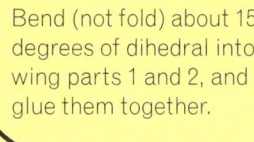

Fold the tabs on the rudder and glue it to the top of the stabilizer.

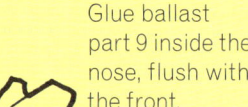

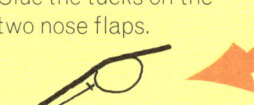

Fold parts 5 and 6 and glue them to the rudder and the bottom of the stabilizer. (photo A)

Bend the fuselage into shape, and glue half of tab 8 inside the nose.

Glue ballast part 9 inside the nose, flush with the front.

Glue the tucks on the two nose flaps.

Glue the remaining half of part 8 inside the nose to close it.

Glue half of tab 10 inside the rear fuselage. Glue the flaps at the bottom of the nose closed. Seal the front point in place with a dab of glue.

Glue the rudder in place. The small round tab fits inside the rear fuselage.

Glue the bottom of the fuselage closed, but leave the very back open for the rudder.

Glue ballast parts 11 to 14 inside the nose, as far forward as possible.

Glue the wing in place, under the front tab and over the side tabs and rear fuselage. Make sure it is straight!

A Glue parts 5 and 6 to the rudder and the bottom of the stabilizer. Make sure they are quite straight!

B Glue the spiked tabs inside the rolled engine parts, up to the dotted line. Bend the spikes inwards just a little.

C Glue the front and back of the engine over the spikes. See the instructions for the direction of the seams.

Cut out the slits in engine brackets 15 and 16, and glue the tucks in each. (photo D)

Slide the brackets onto the wings, center them over the alignment marks, and fasten them in place with beads of glue on the top and bottom. (photo E)

Glue engine part 17 into a tube.

Glue a spiked tab inside each end, up to the dotted line. Bend the spikes inward slightly. (photo B)

Glue the fronts and backs over the spike tabs. Note the directions of the seams. (photo C)

Make cones for the front and back of the engines.

Glue the engines to their brackets, with the main seam at the top, and the front of the bracket flush with the front of the tube. (photo F)

Make a second engine from parts 22 to 26.

Glue the tucks in part 27 to make the canopy.

Glue the hook parts together.

Glue the canopy in place.

This is how it will look.

Glue the hook to the bottom of the nose at the mark, and you're finished!

D Glue the tucks at both ends of the engine brackets.

E Glue the brackets in place over the marks on the wings. Beads of glue on the top and bottom will hold it in place.

F This is how the engines are attached to the brackets.

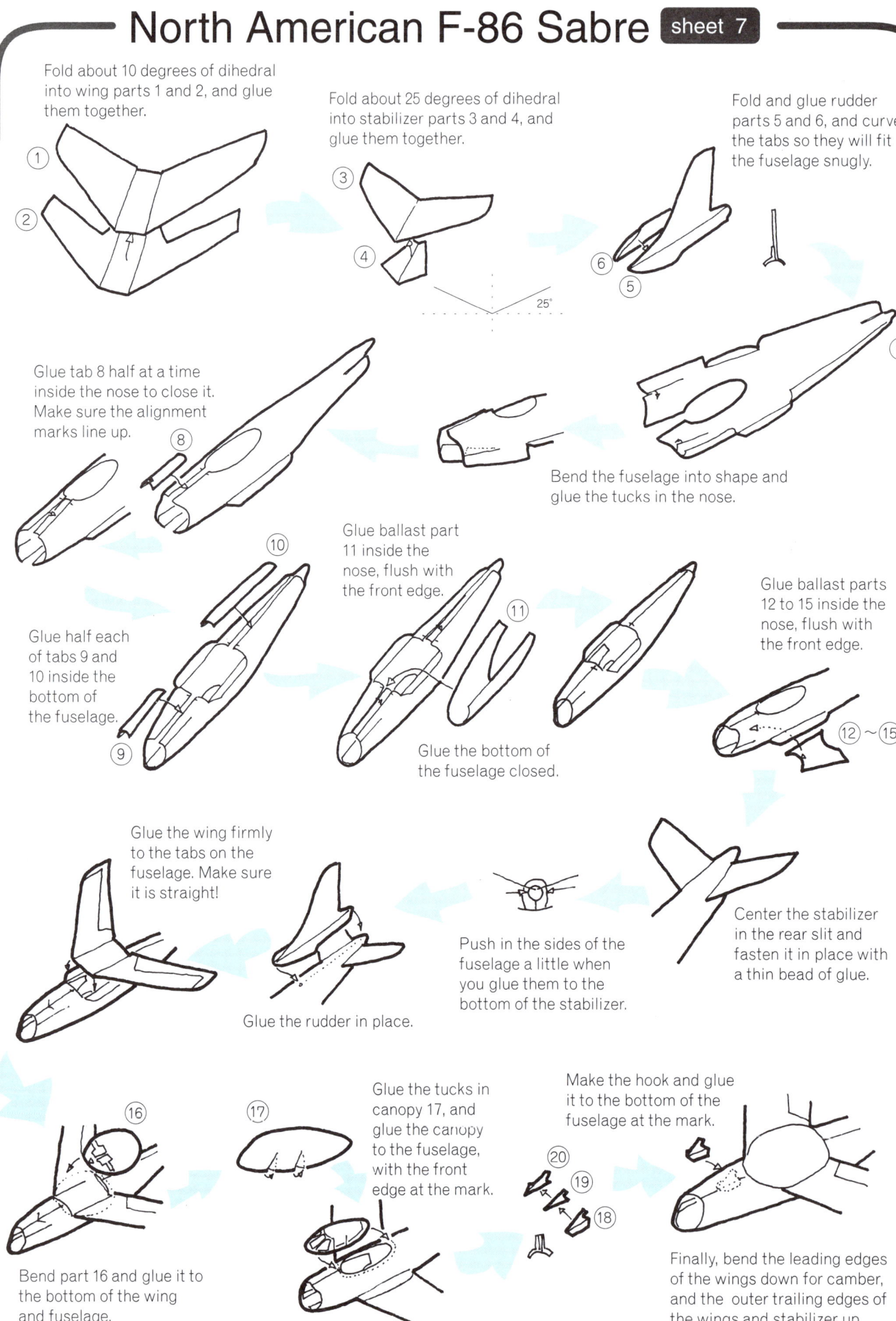

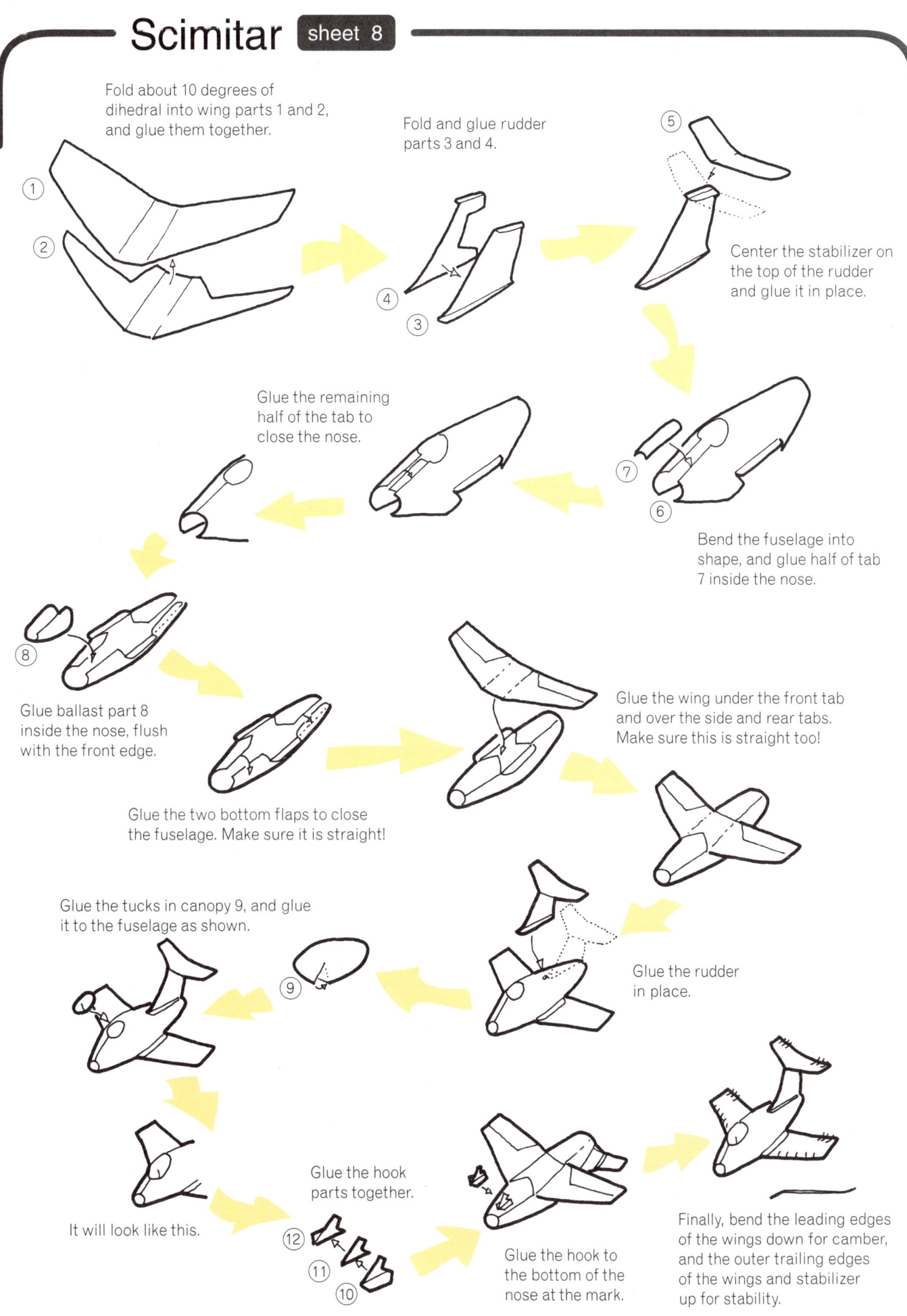

Northrop B-49 sheets 9-10

Roll and glue ballast parts 1 to 6 into four rolls. (photo A)

Carefully crease the leading edge of each wing just enough that it forms a sharp V shape as shown. Cut out the slits on the trailing edge, put a thin bead of glue along the inside edge, and glue the very back closed. The wing should be about half an inch thick. (photo B)

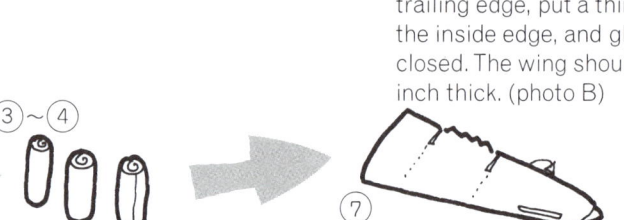

Place the wing face up on a table, and while holding the trailing edge, push down the front corner as shown.

Before the glue dries completely, look along the trailing edge to make sure it is straight. If not, straighten it carefully.

The finished wing will look like this from the top and bottom.

Glue tabs 9 and 10 inside the wings as shown, up to the dotted line. Part 9 goes on the top of the left wing, and part 10 goes on the bottom of the right wing.

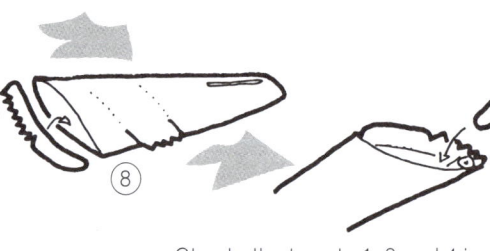

Glue ballast parts 1, 3 and 4 inside the leading edge of the left wing as shown. Don't force them so far forward that they change the shape of the wing. Repeat this step for the right wing. (photo C)

Carefully glue the two wing halves together, with the tabs inside each wing. The top and bottom seams should meet exactly, and the wing will still be about half an inch thick. Don't squash the wing! (photo D)

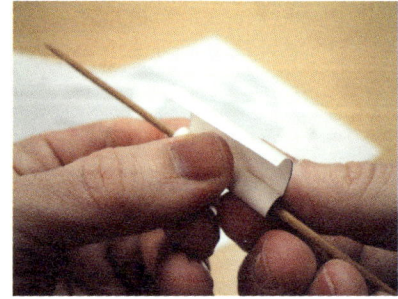

A Roll the ballast tightly around a toothpick or skewer, glue it closed, and remove the skewer.

B Line up the trailing edges carefully, and glue only the very edge.

C Glue two ballast rolls inside the leading edge of each wing.

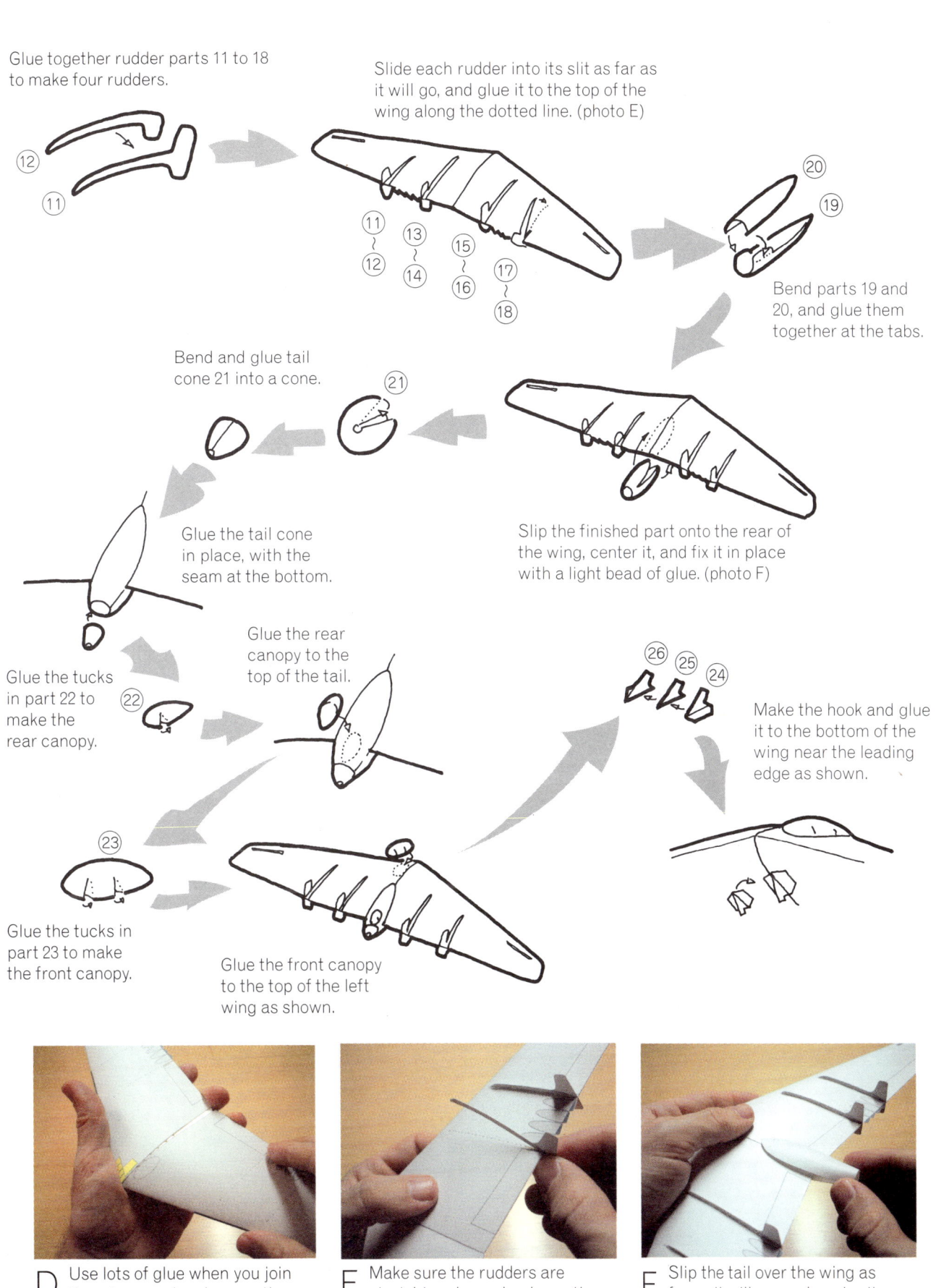

Glue together rudder parts 11 to 18 to make four rudders.

Slide each rudder into its slit as far as it will go, and glue it to the top of the wing along the dotted line. (photo E)

Bend parts 19 and 20, and glue them together at the tabs.

Bend and glue tail cone 21 into a cone.

Slip the finished part onto the rear of the wing, center it, and fix it in place with a light bead of glue. (photo F)

Glue the tail cone in place, with the seam at the bottom.

Glue the rear canopy to the top of the tail.

Glue the tucks in part 22 to make the rear canopy.

Make the hook and glue it to the bottom of the wing near the leading edge as shown.

Glue the tucks in part 23 to make the front canopy.

Glue the front canopy to the top of the left wing as shown.

D Use lots of glue when you join the wings, and make sure the edges meet exactly.

E Make sure the rudders are straight and are glued exactly over the dotted lines.

F Slip the tail over the wing as far as it will go, and center it carefully before gluing.

Avro CF-105 Arrow — sheet 11

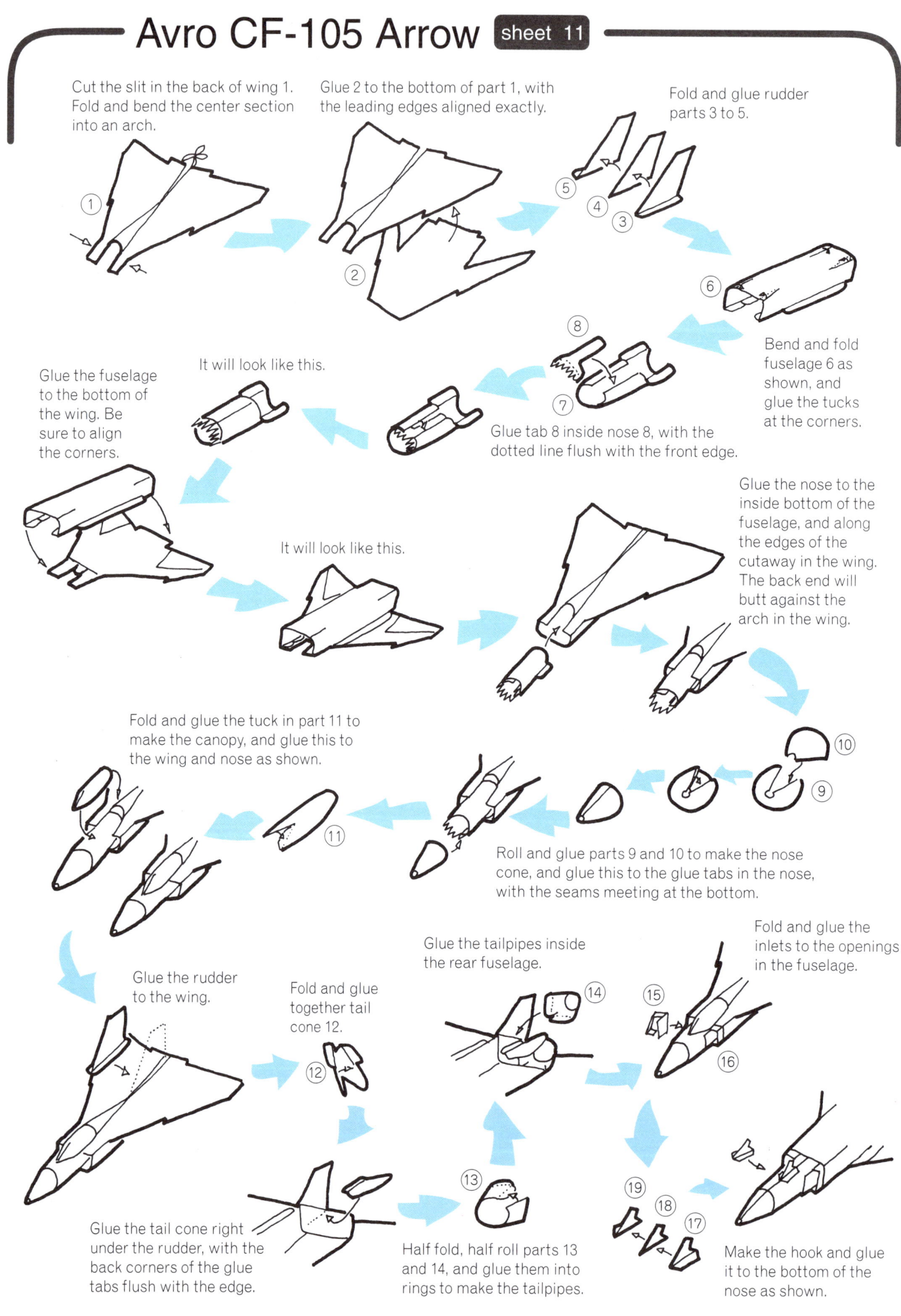

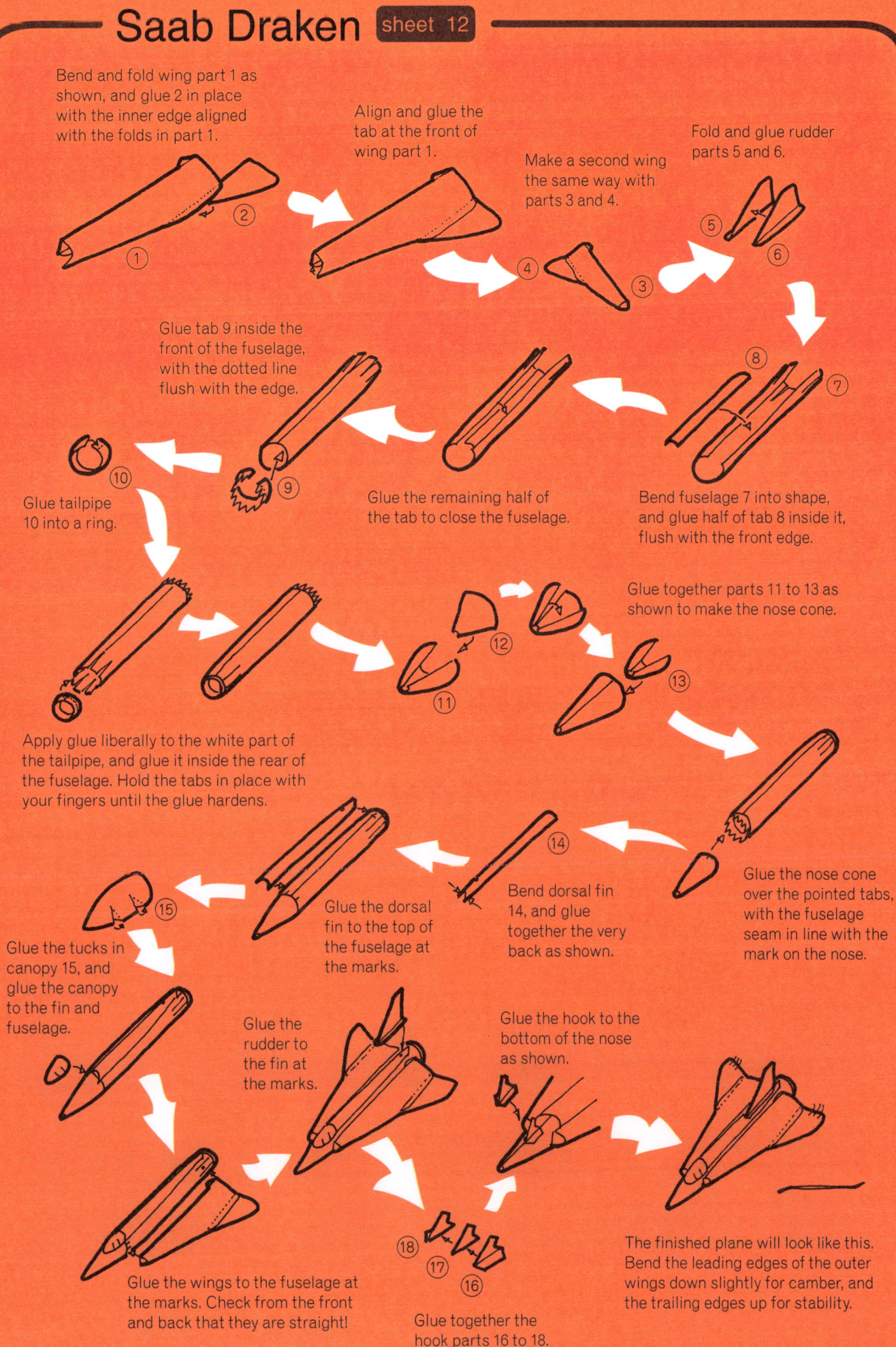

Lockheed F-104 Starfighter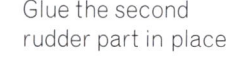

Fold and glue parts 1 to 4 to make the two wings.

 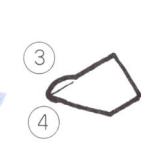

Fold the tabs on rudder part 5. Glue part 6 to the inner side, with enough room between it and the tab to insert a piece of paper.

Glue the second rudder part in place.

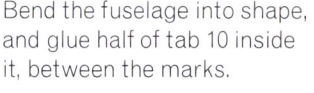

Bend the fuselage into shape, and glue half of tab 10 inside it, between the marks.

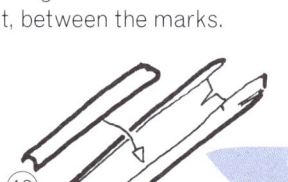

Glue stabilizer 8 in place. Fasten part 6 to it with a thin bead of glue.

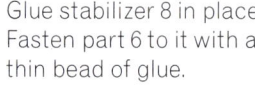
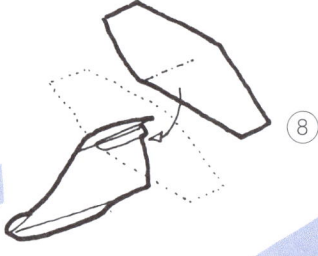

Carefully curve the points at the front of the fuselage, butt them together, and glue them in place one at a time. Hold them carefully until the glue takes hold. (photo A)

Glue the fuselage bottom together. Line up the marks carefully to avoid twisting! (photo C)

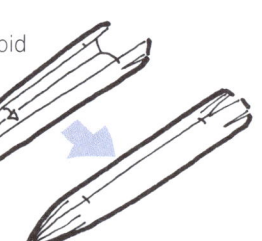

Seal the seams with glue.

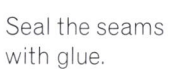

Glue ballast parts 11 and 12 inside the nose. (photo B)

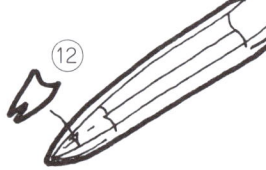

Glue the tailpipe into a ring.

Apply glue liberally to the white part of the tailpipe, and glue it inside the rear of the fuselage. Hold the tabs in place with your fingers until the glue hardens. (photo D)

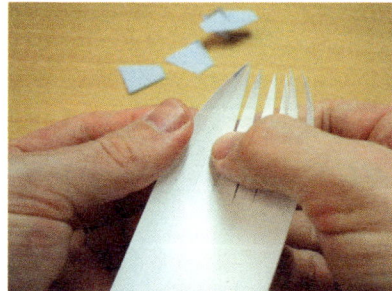

A The points in the nose fit together neatly if you curve them before gluing. Hold them in place gently.

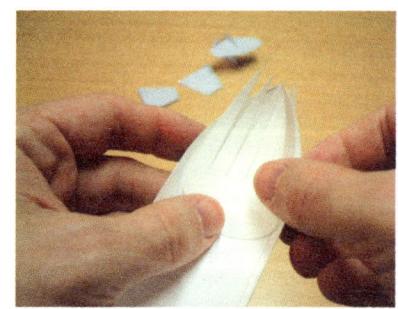

B The ballast is also reinforcement, so glue all of the points thoroughly.

C Be sure the alignment marks are lined up or the fuselage will be twisted.

Bend the two inlets 14 and 15 into shape, and glue them to the fuselage with their corners exactly over the marks. (photo E)

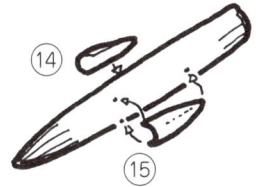

Glue the wings exactly over the lines on the inlets. Check them carefully from the front and rear to make sure they are straight. (photo F)

Glue the tail to the fuselage at the mark. Make sure it is straight too.

Bend and glue the inlet cones 16 and 17 in the center of the inlets, just inside the opening.

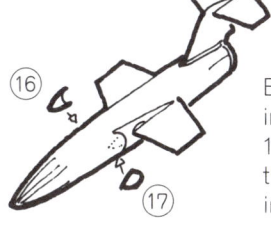

Glue the tucks in part 18 to make the canopy.

Glue the canopy to the fuselage, with the back at the mark.

Make the hook and glue it to the bottom of the fuselage, with the back edge about half an inch ahead of the mark.

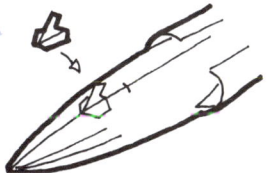

Add camber to the wings for lift, and bend up the trailing edge of the stabilizer slightly for stability.

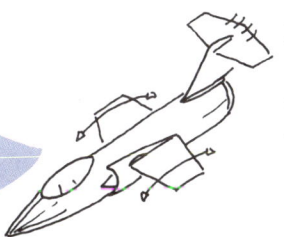

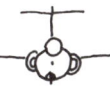

It will look like this from the front, with about 5 degrees of dihedral.

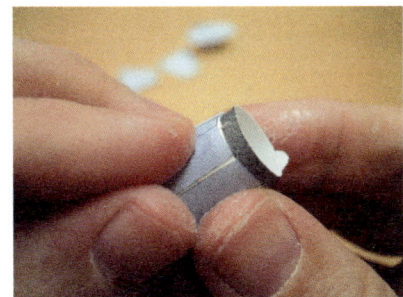

D Hold the tabs of the rear fuselage around the tailpipe until the glue grips.

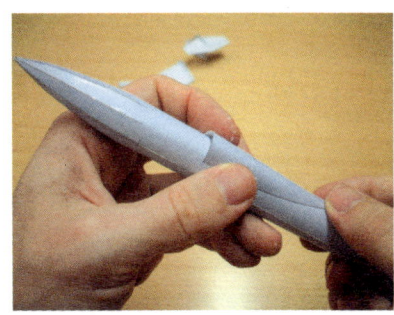

E Bend the inlets into shape, and glue the corners exactly over the marks on the fuselage.

F Glue the wings exactly over the lines on the inlets, and check from the front and rear that they are straight.

Northrop F-5 Tiger sheet 14

Fold about 10 degrees of dihedral into wing parts 1 and 2, and glue them together.

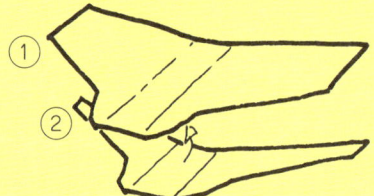

Glue stabilizer parts 3 and 4 together.

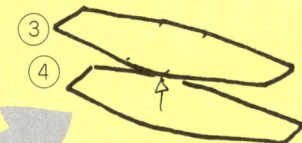

Fold and glue rudder parts 5 to 7.

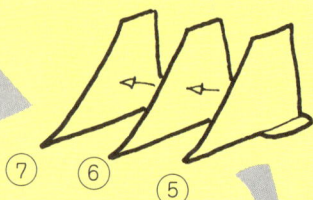

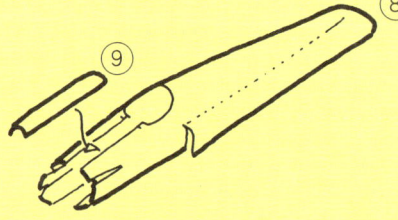

Bend and fold the fuselage as shown. Glue half of tab 9 inside the nose.

Glue the remaining half of the tab to close the nose.

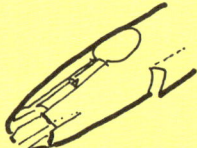

Glue the tucks in the nose.

It will look like this from the front.

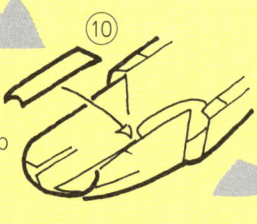

Glue half of tab 10 inside the bottom of the nose.

Glue ballast part 11 inside the nose, with the dotted line at the front edge.

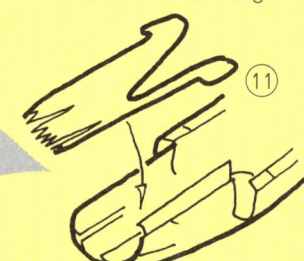

Glue the stabilizer to the fuselage in the same way as the wing. (photo D)

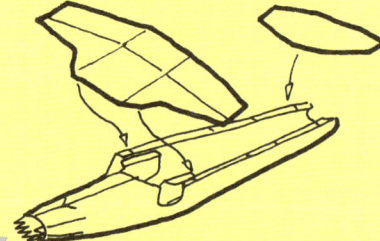

Glue the wing to the tabs on the bottom of the fuselage, between the marks. Line up the corners of the fuselage with the fold lines in the wing. (photo B)

Glue the remaining half of 10 to close the fuselage bottom. (photo A)

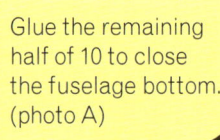

It will now look like this from the front.

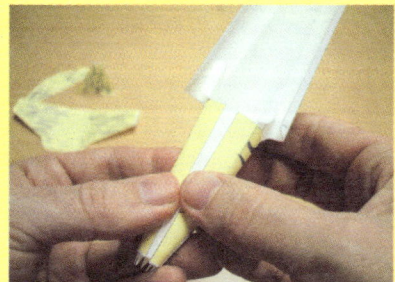

A Butt the two edges of the fuselage bottom together when you join them.

B Match the corners and alignment marks with the fold lines and edges of the wing.

C Tweezers help when gluing the tabs on part 11 to the wing.

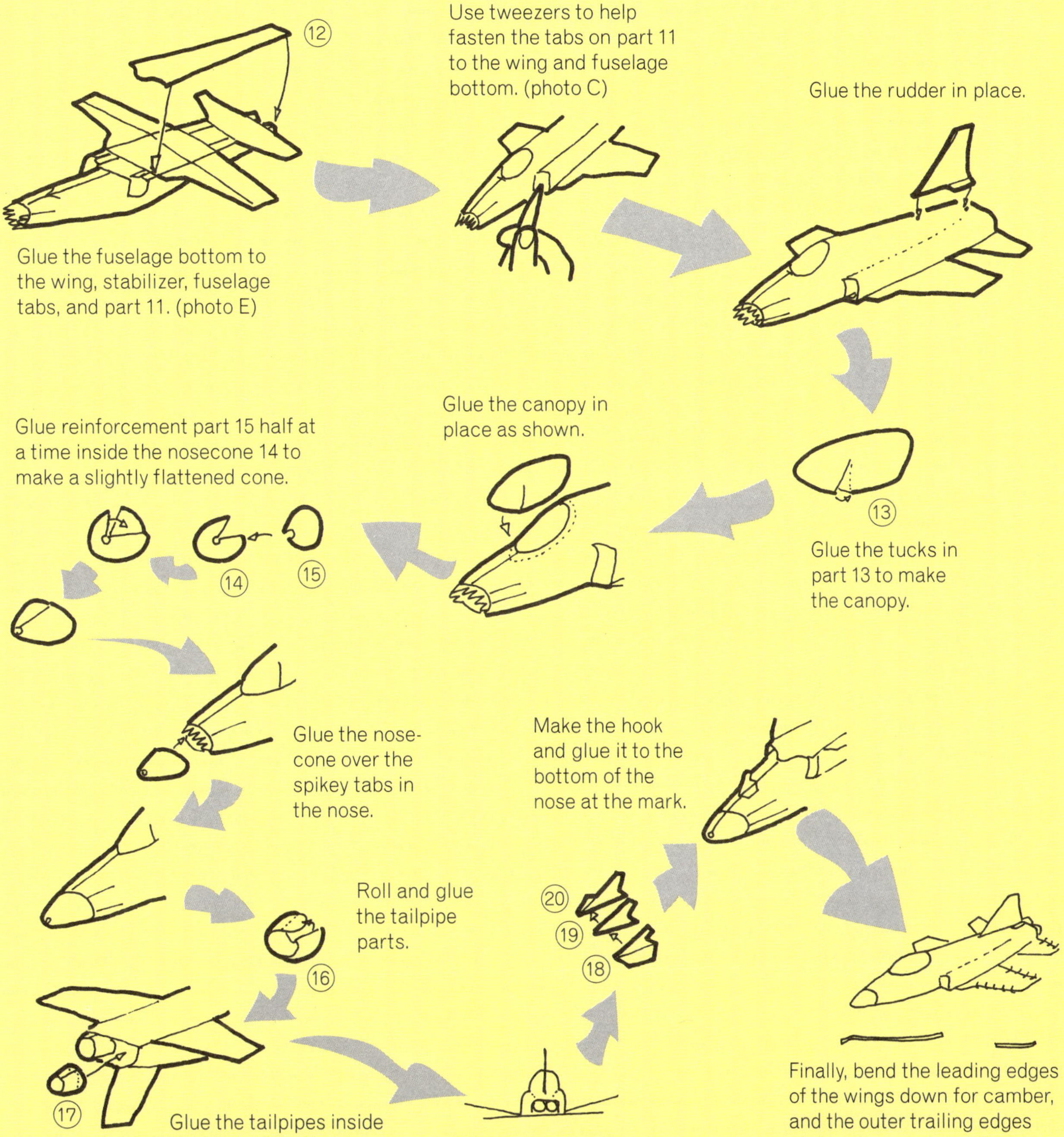

Glue the fuselage bottom to the wing, stabilizer, fuselage tabs, and part 11. (photo E)

⑫

Use tweezers to help fasten the tabs on part 11 to the wing and fuselage bottom. (photo C)

Glue the rudder in place.

⑬

Glue the tucks in part 13 to make the canopy.

Glue the canopy in place as shown.

Glue reinforcement part 15 half at a time inside the nosecone 14 to make a slightly flattened cone.

⑭ ⑮

Glue the nosecone over the spikey tabs in the nose.

Make the hook and glue it to the bottom of the nose at the mark.

⑱ ⑲ ⑳

Roll and glue the tailpipe parts.

⑯

⑰ Glue the tailpipes inside the back of the fuselage as shown. (photo F)

This is how it will look from the back.

Finally, bend the leading edges of the wings down for camber, and the outer trailing edges of the wings and stabilizer up for stability.

D Glue the stabilizer to the bottom of the fuselage as you did the wing.

E Glue the fuselage bottom in place. Work quickly or the glue will dry before you get it fixed in place.

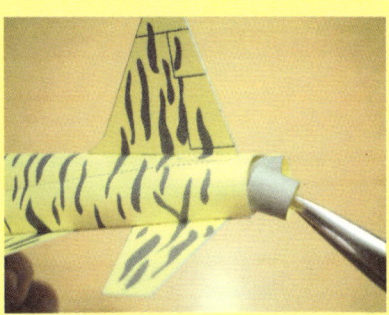

F About a quarter to a third of the tailpipes will stick out when you glue them inside the tail.

61

Grumman X-29 sheet 15

Fold about 10 degrees of dihedral into wing parts 1 to 3 and glue them together.

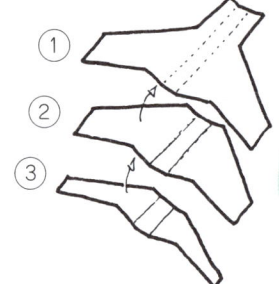

Fold and glue together the rudder, and canards as shown.

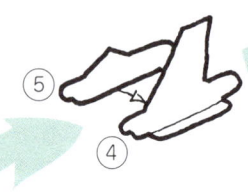

Bend the fuselage into shape, and glue half of tab 11 inside the nose.

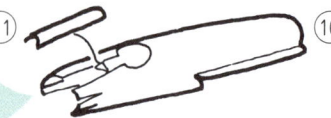

Glue the tucks in the nose.

Glue half of tab 12 inside the bottom of the nose.

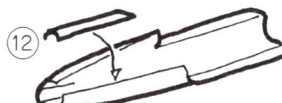

Glue the nose closed.

Glue ballast part 13 inside the nose, with the dotted line flush with the front edge.

Glue the fuselage bottom closed.

Glue the wing under the front tabs and over the side tabs. The corners of the fuselage will meet the folds in the wing.

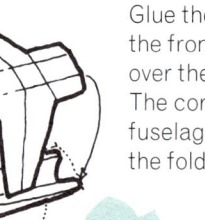

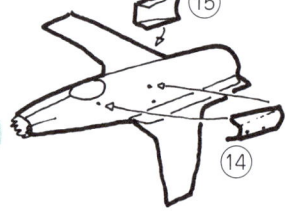

Fold inlets 14 and 15 into shape, and glue them to the fuselage sides, with the corners exactly over the marks.

Glue the canards and rudder in place as shown. Make sure they are over the marks, and check from the front that they are straight!

Make the nose cone from parts 16 and 17, and glue it over the nose tabs with the seam at the bottom.

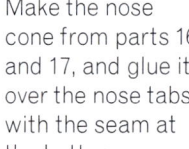

Glue the tucks in the canopy, and glue it to the fuselage with the front edge at the alignment mark.

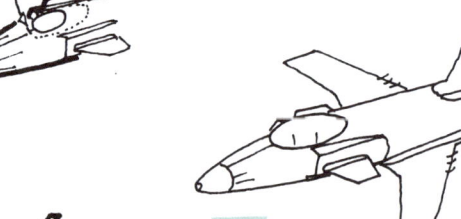

Glue tailpipe 19 into a ring.

Glue the pointy tabs inside the back of the fuselage and to the wing, with the seam at the bottom.

Make the hook and glue it under the nose at the mark.

Bend up the trailing edge and back corner of the wing very slightly as shown for stability.

62

Lockheed F-117 Nighthawk sheet 16

Fold and glue wing 1 as shown.

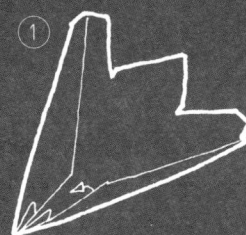

Glue the hook as well. Press the wing bottom up between sheets of scrap paper under a heavy book (with the hook sticking out!) until it dries.

Fold and glue rudder parts 2 and 3.

Lightly crease the fuselage along the mountain and valley fold lines, and glue the nose together as shown.

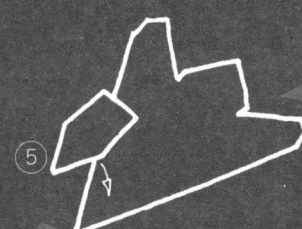

Here's how it will look.

Glue ballast parts 5 to 9 to the upper side of the wing. Stagger the pieces backwards very slightly to leave room for the sloping fuselage.

Glue the rear three tabs on each side of the fuselage to the top of the wing as shown, with the rear edges aligned.

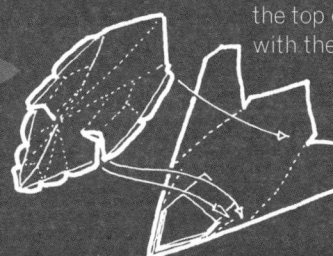

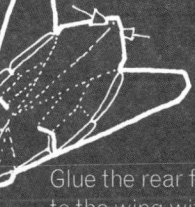

Glue the rear fuselage to the wing with a bead of glue. Lay the wing on a table while doing this to be sure it is straight.

Glue the intakes in place over the openings on each side of the fuselage.

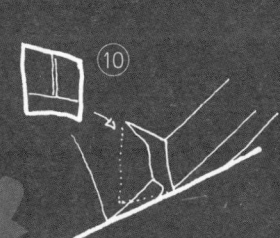

Glue the front tabs to the bottom of the wing.

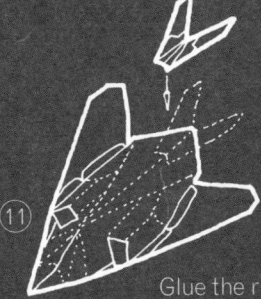

Glue the rudder to the top of the fuselage, flush with the rear edge.

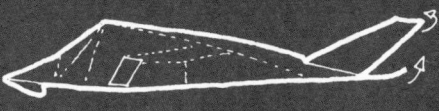

From the side it will look like this. Bend the wingtips up and the rudders inwards slightly for stability.

Fly Your Planes!

I always think that an airplane isn't an airplane if it doesn't fly. You've built your paper models, and they look great, but now it's time to turn them into real airplanes! Carefully carry your planes to a nice big field with soft grass to cushion the landings, on a calm, dry day, and go through a few test flights first. Get used to the way the airplane flies before you begin to "expand the envelope." And always keep safety in mind.

Looking good! Now that's an airplane!

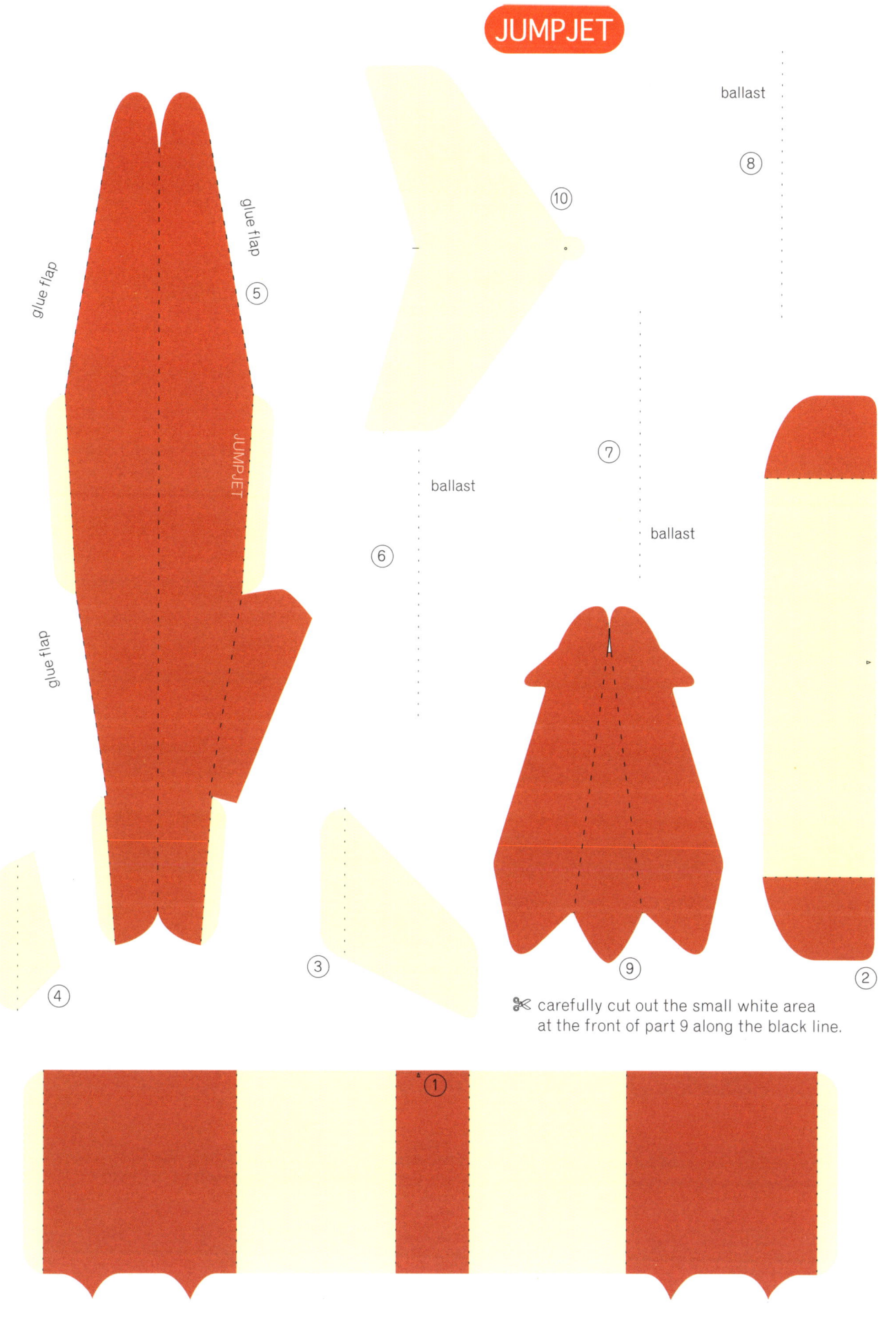

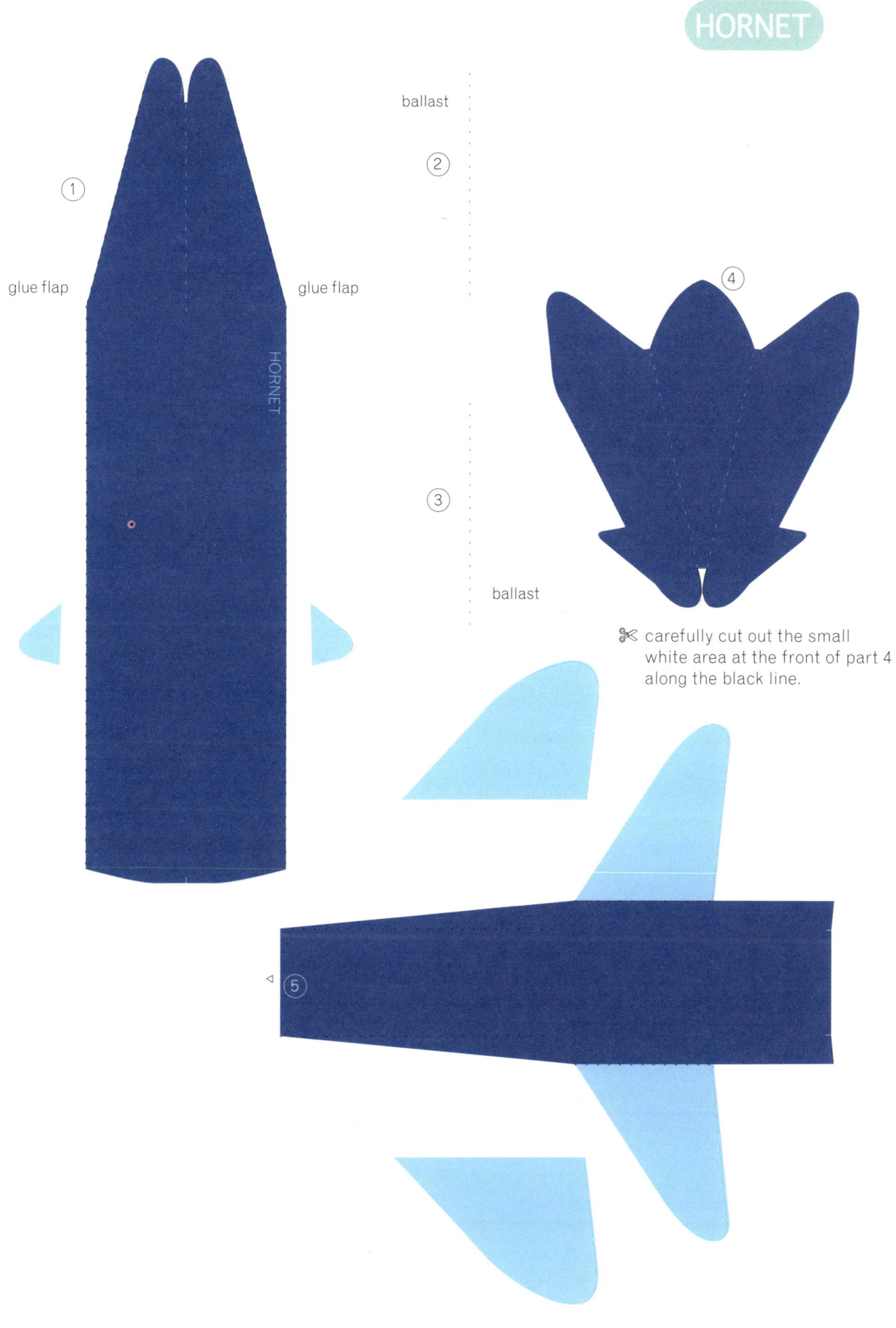

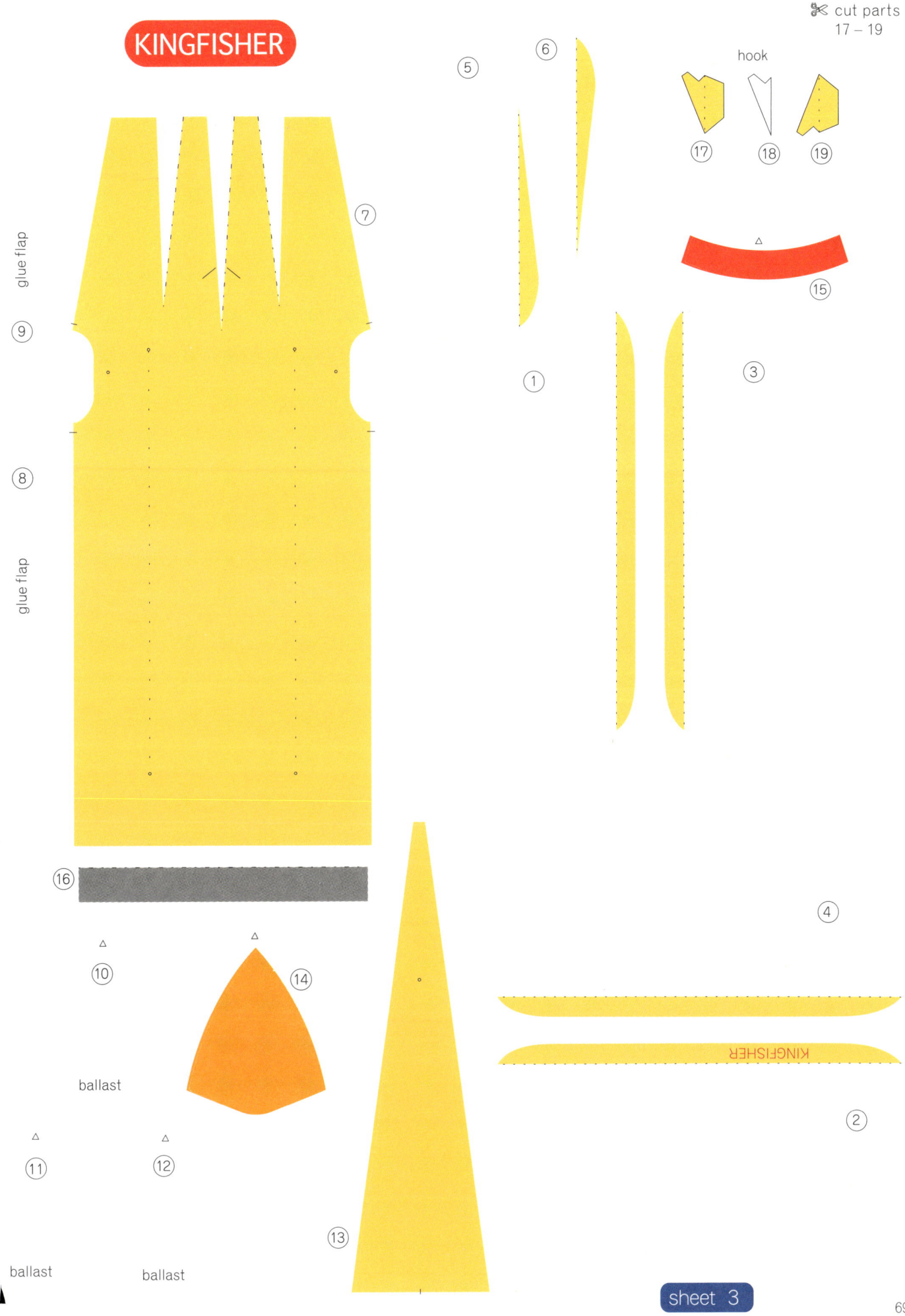

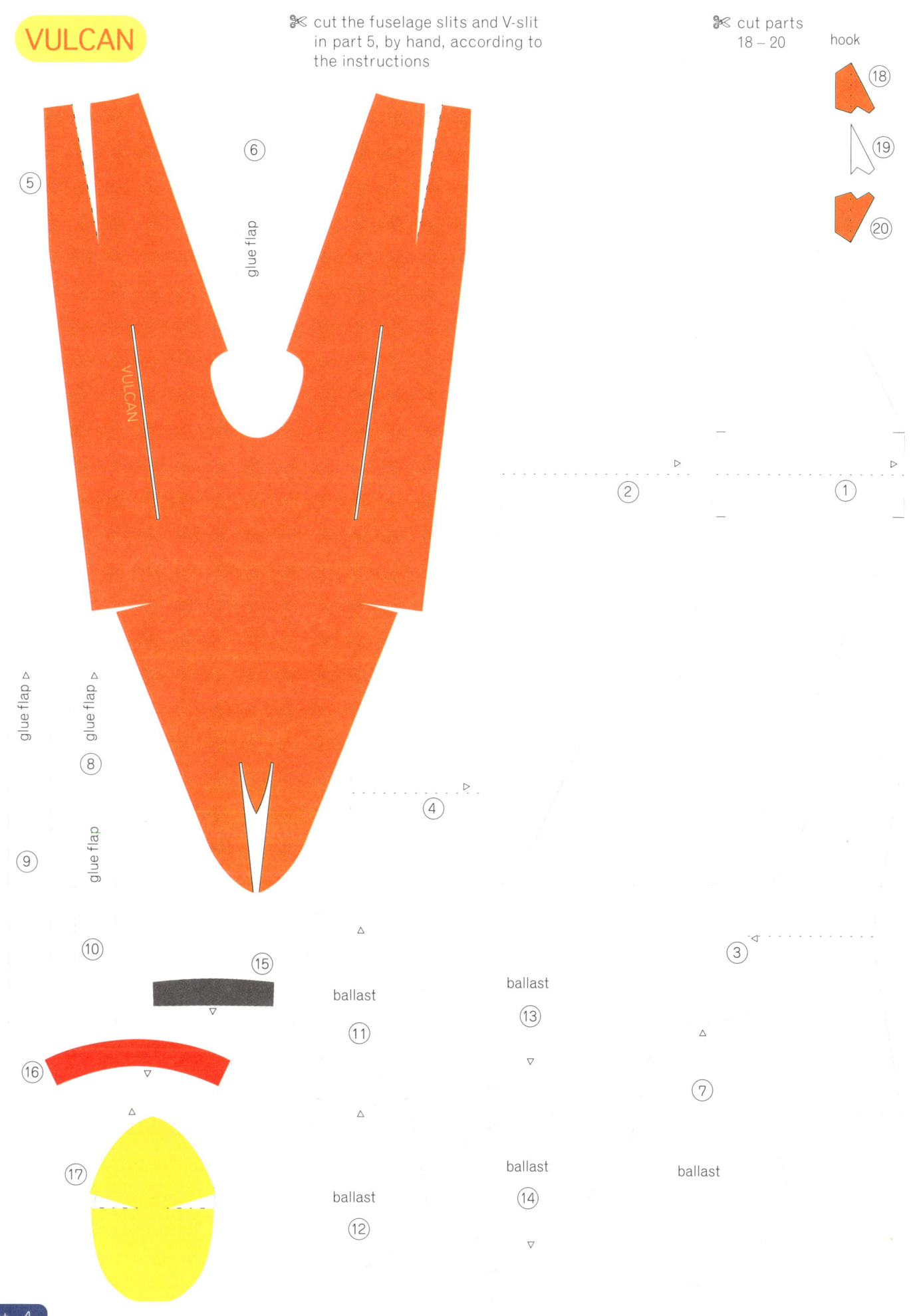

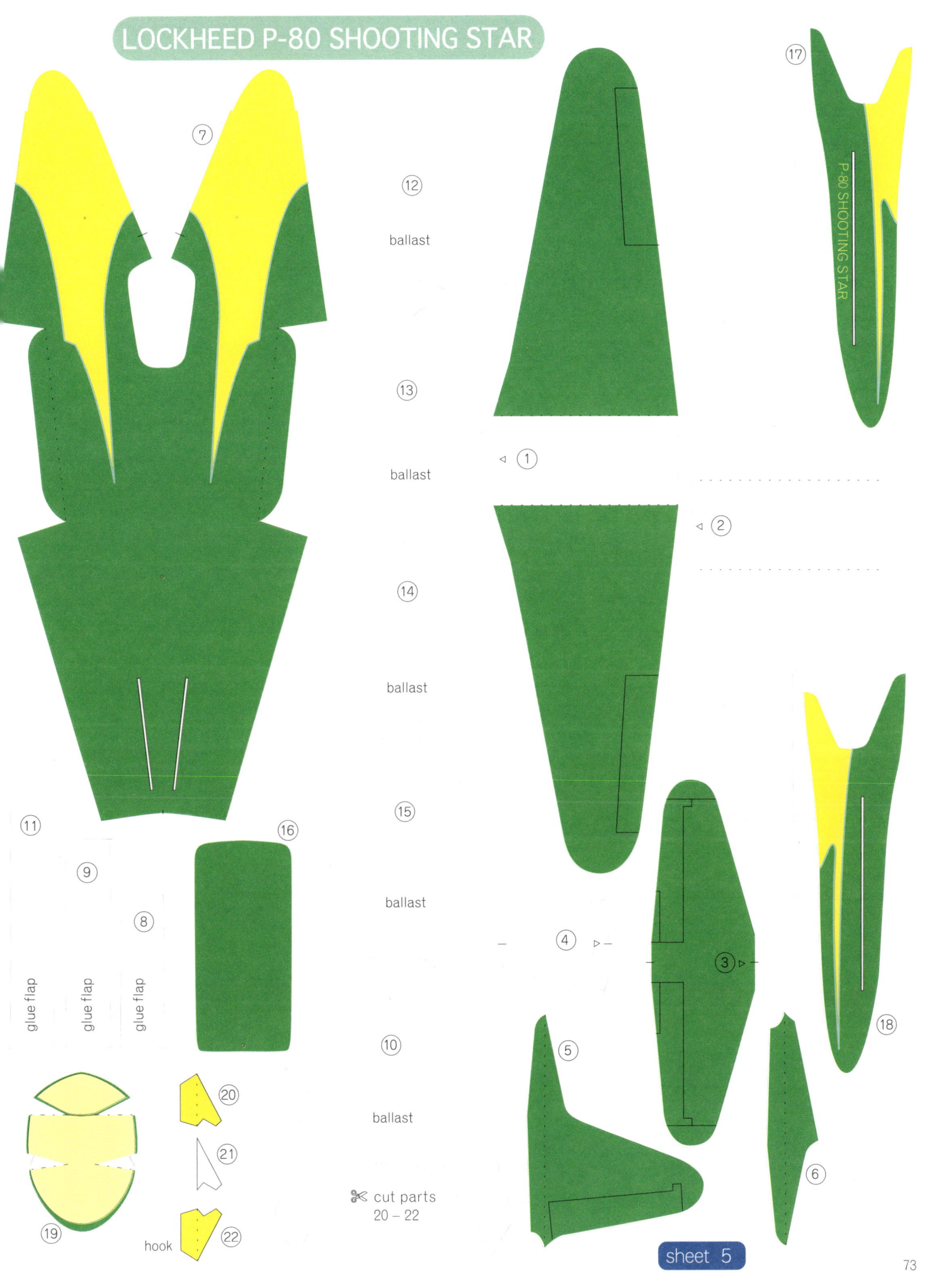

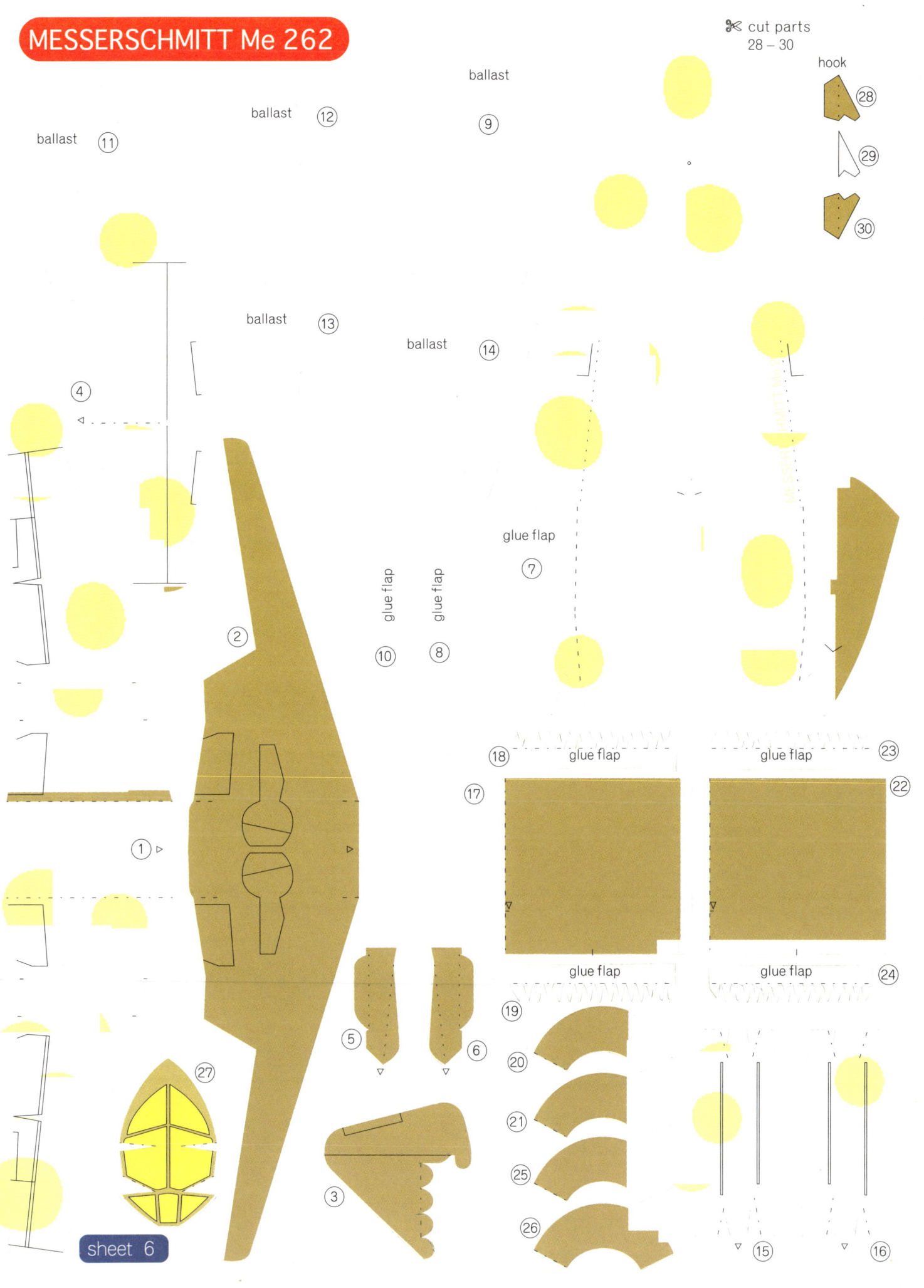

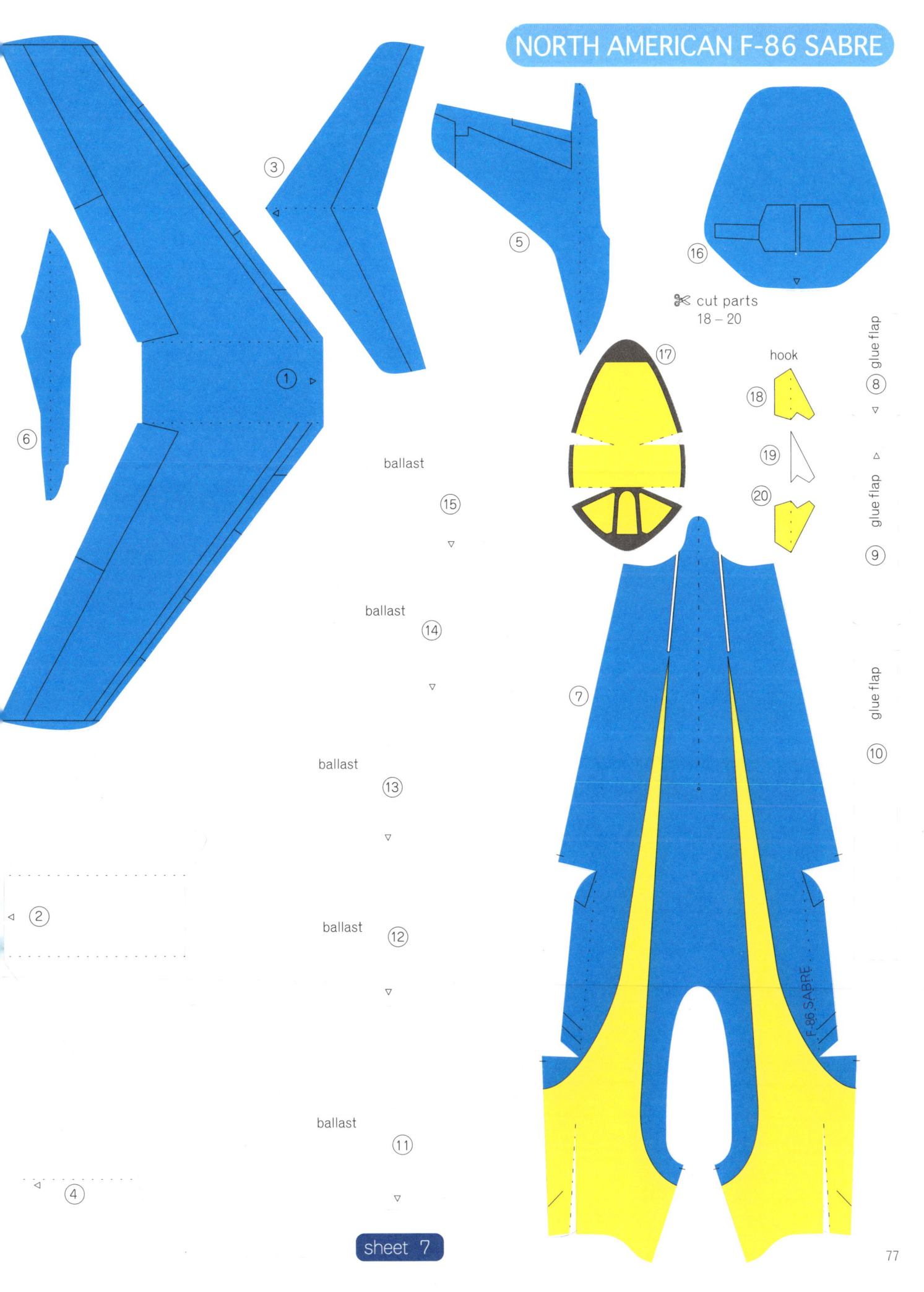

SCIMITAR

cut parts
10 – 12
hook
glue flap
7
glue flap
6
10
11
12
SCIMITAR
1
8
ballast
2
5
9
4
3

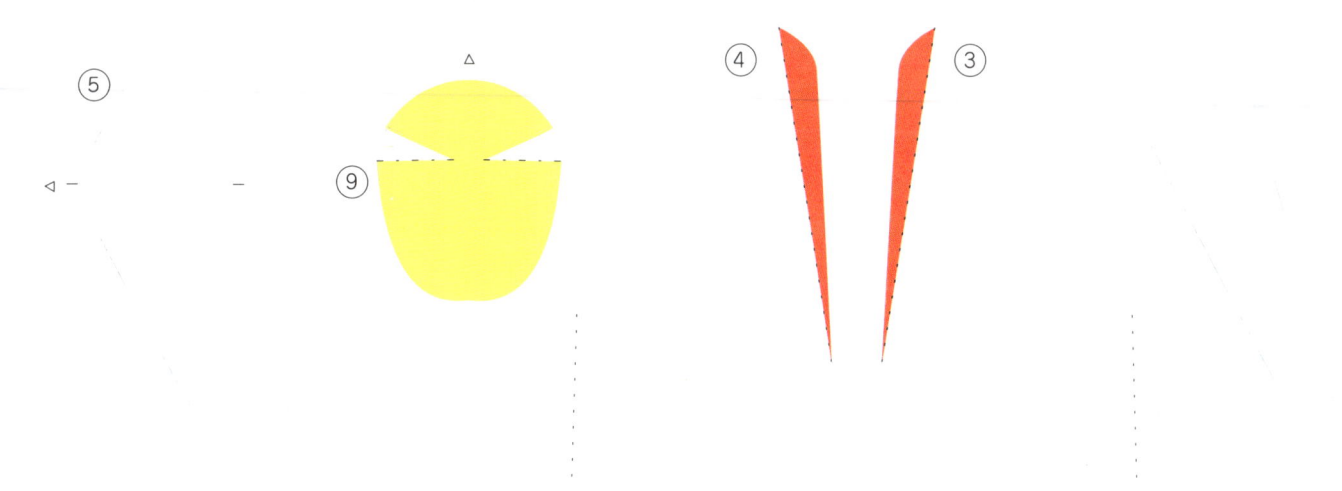

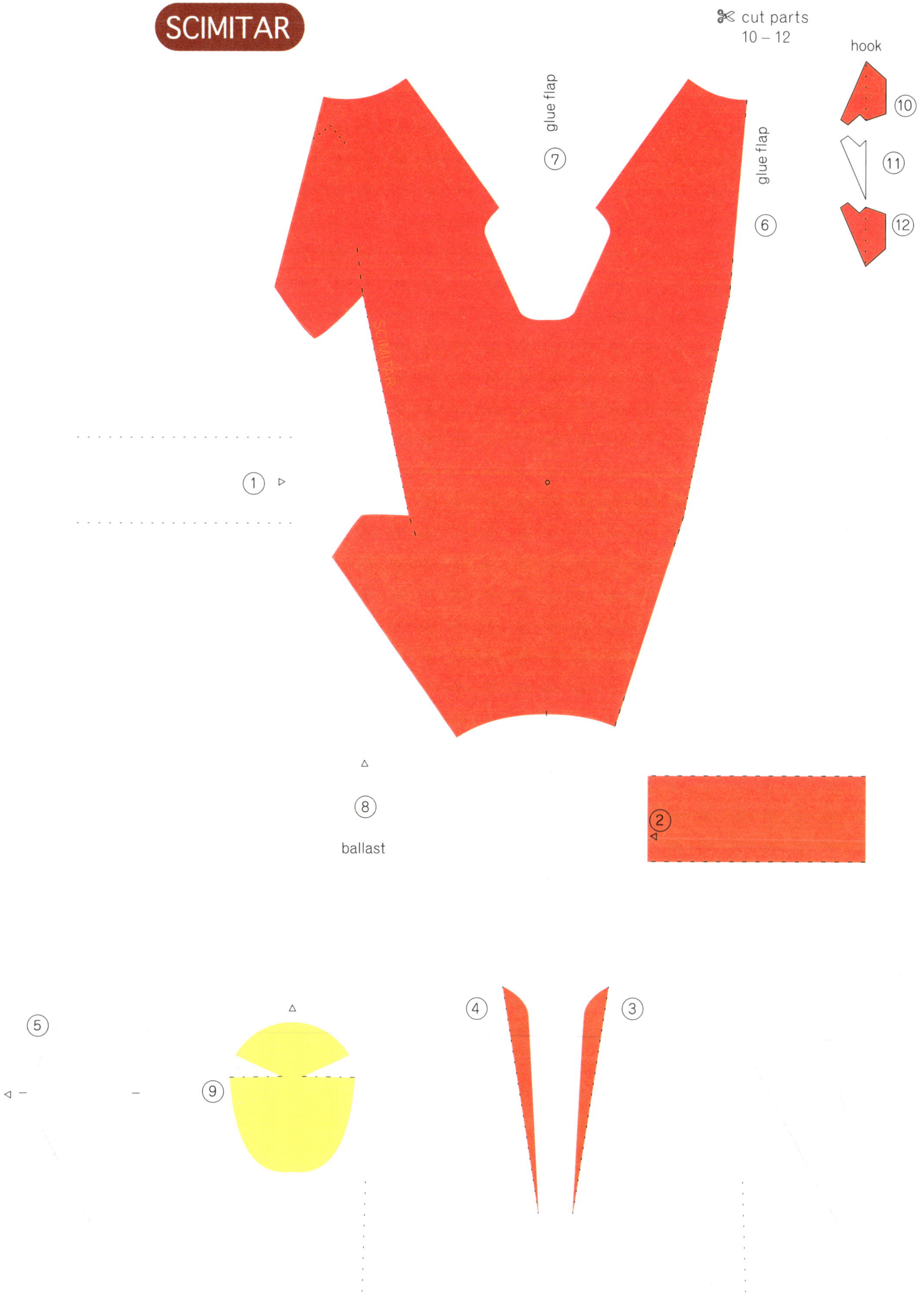

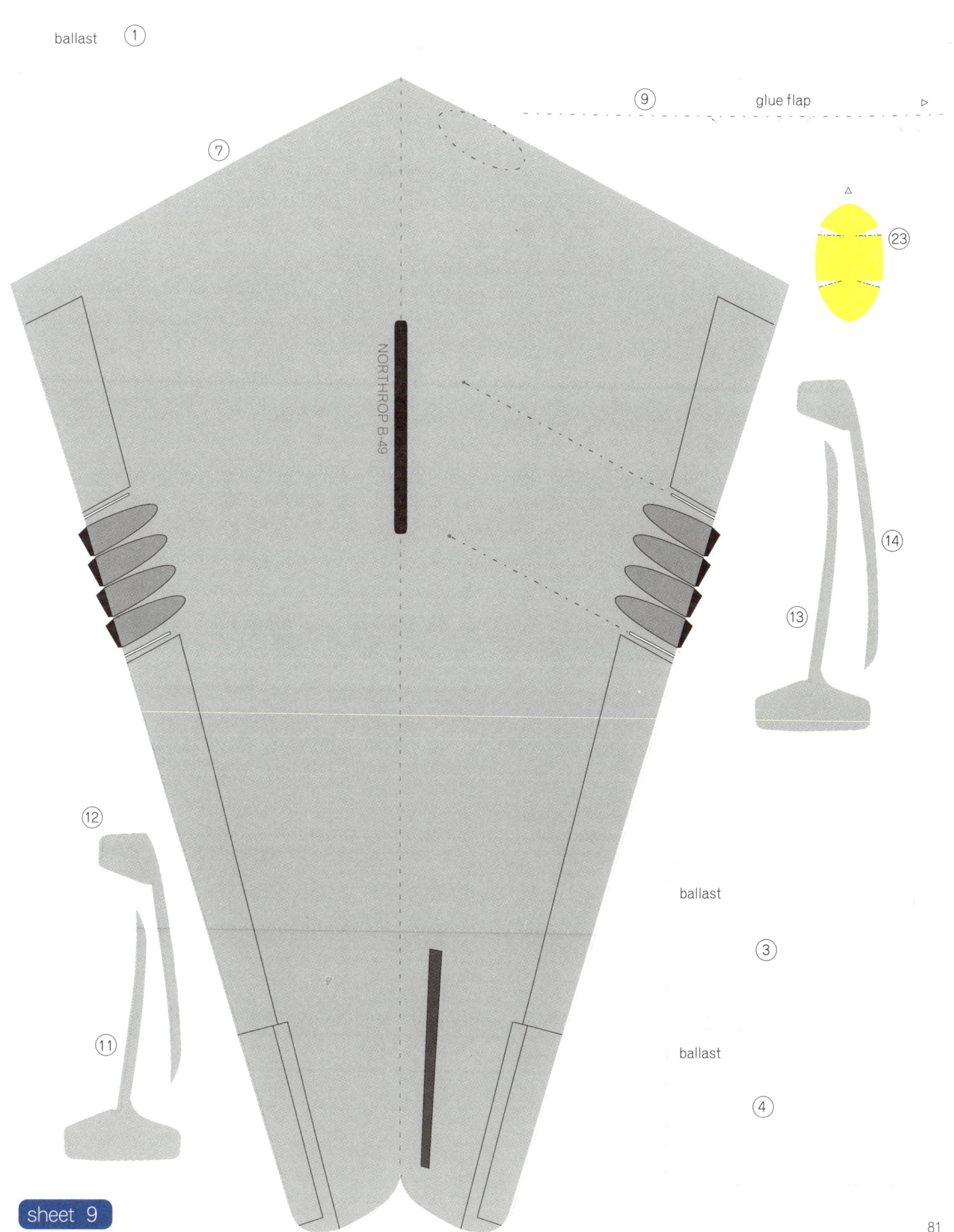

82

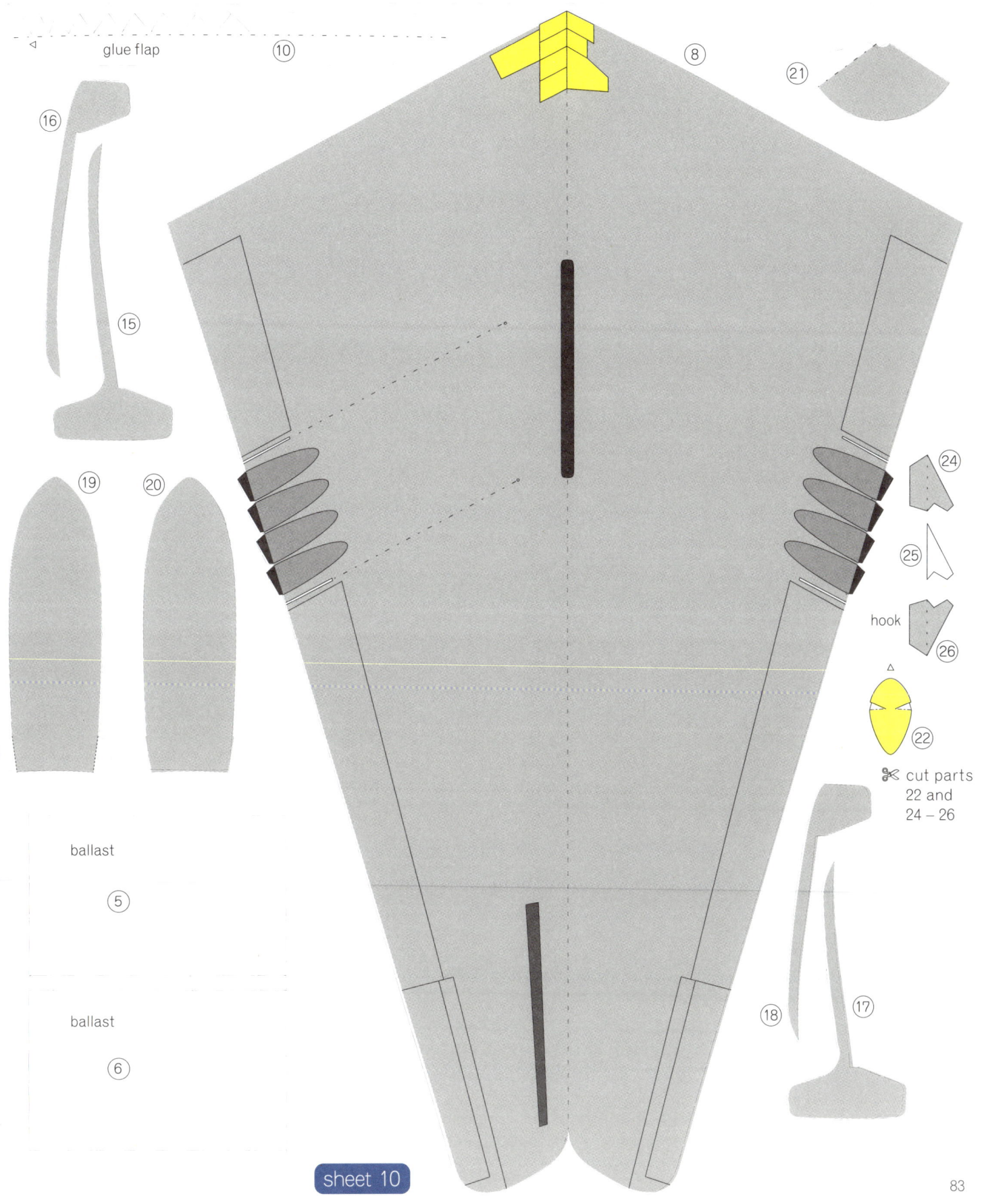

AVRO CF-105 ARROW

✂ cut parts
17 – 19

hook

glue flap

sheet 11

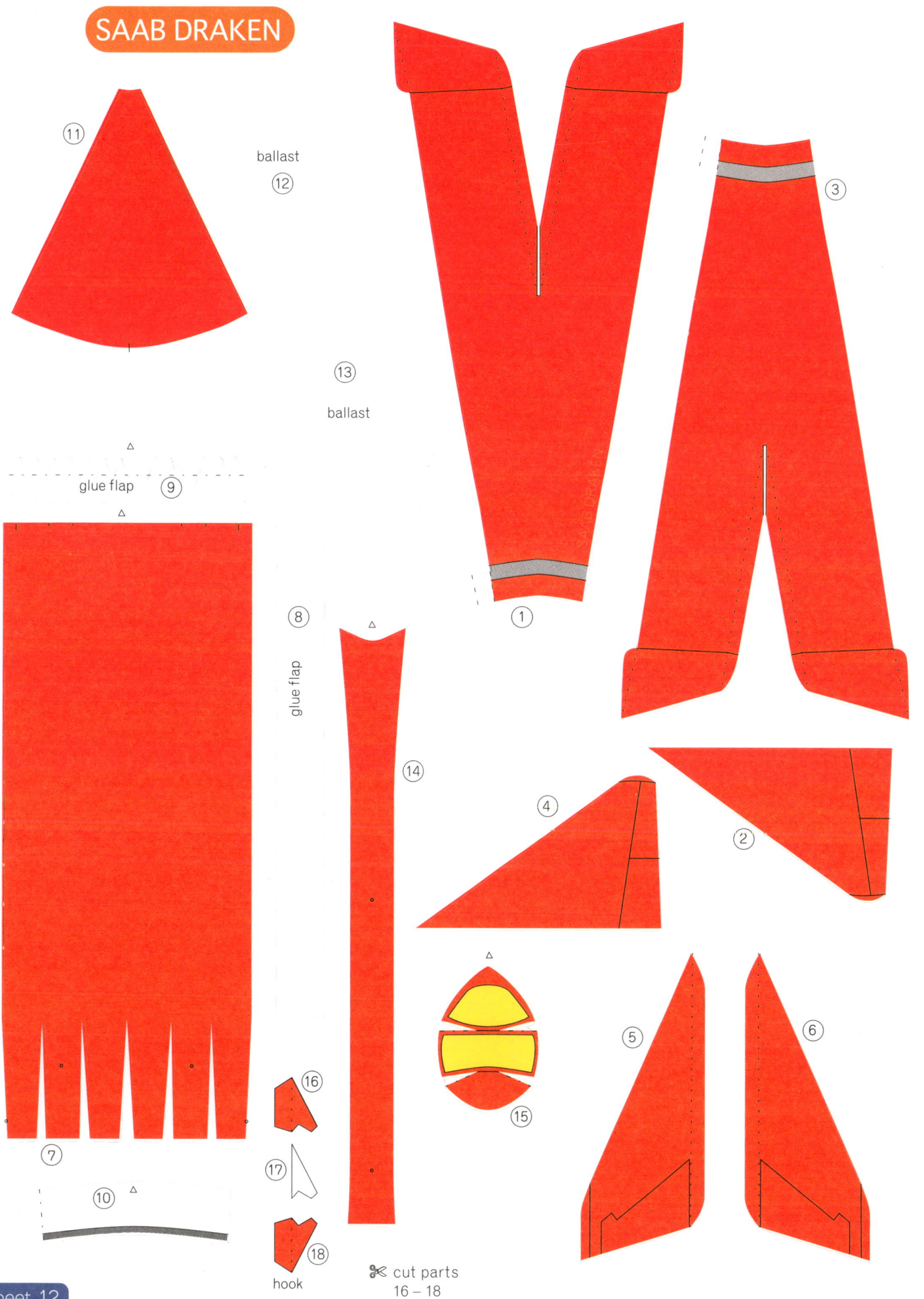

LOCKHEED F-104 STARFIGHTER

cut parts 6, 16 and 17

ballast (11)

ballast (12)

glue flap (10)

cut parts 19 – 21

hook

LOCKHEED F-104 STARFIGHTER

sheet 13

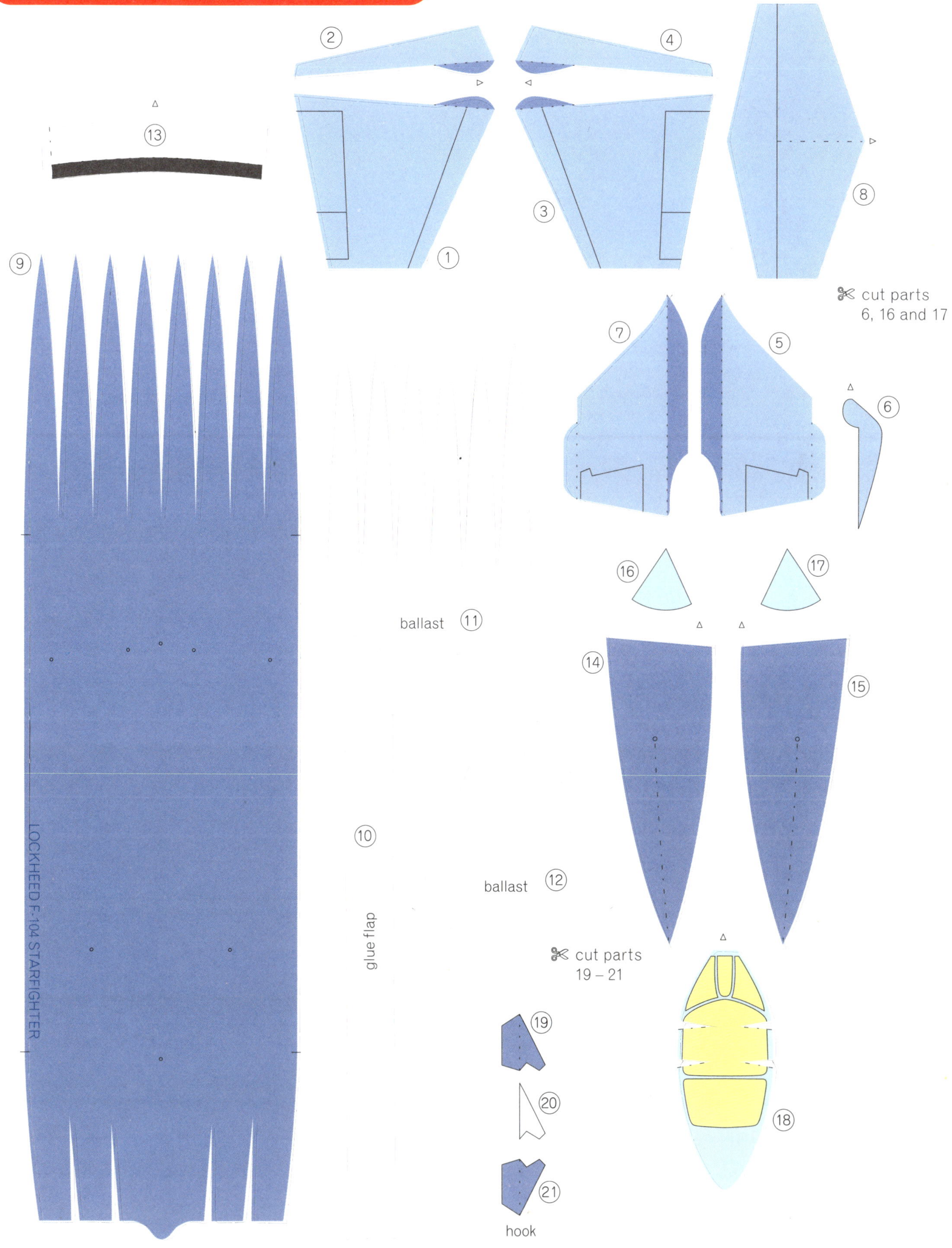

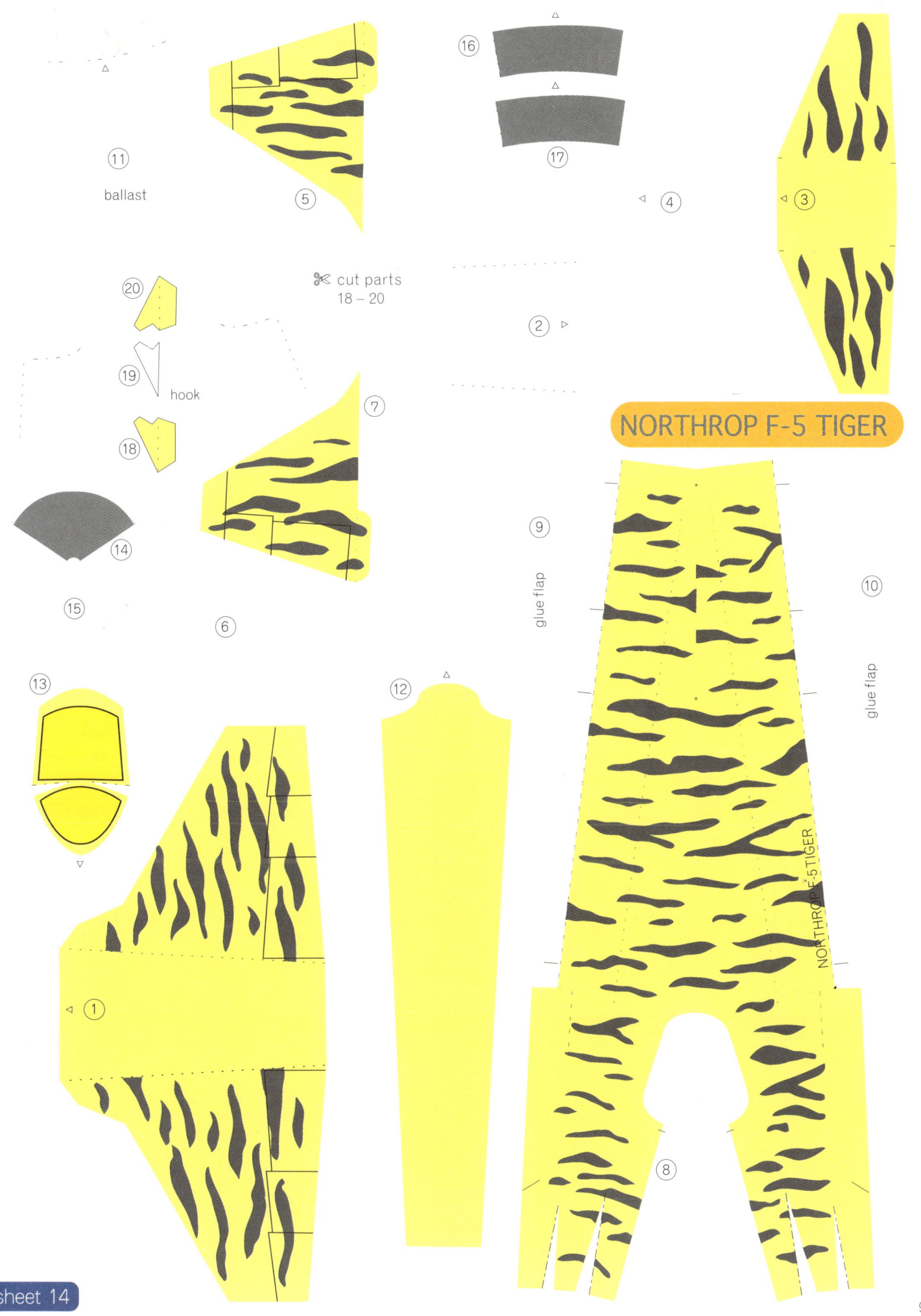

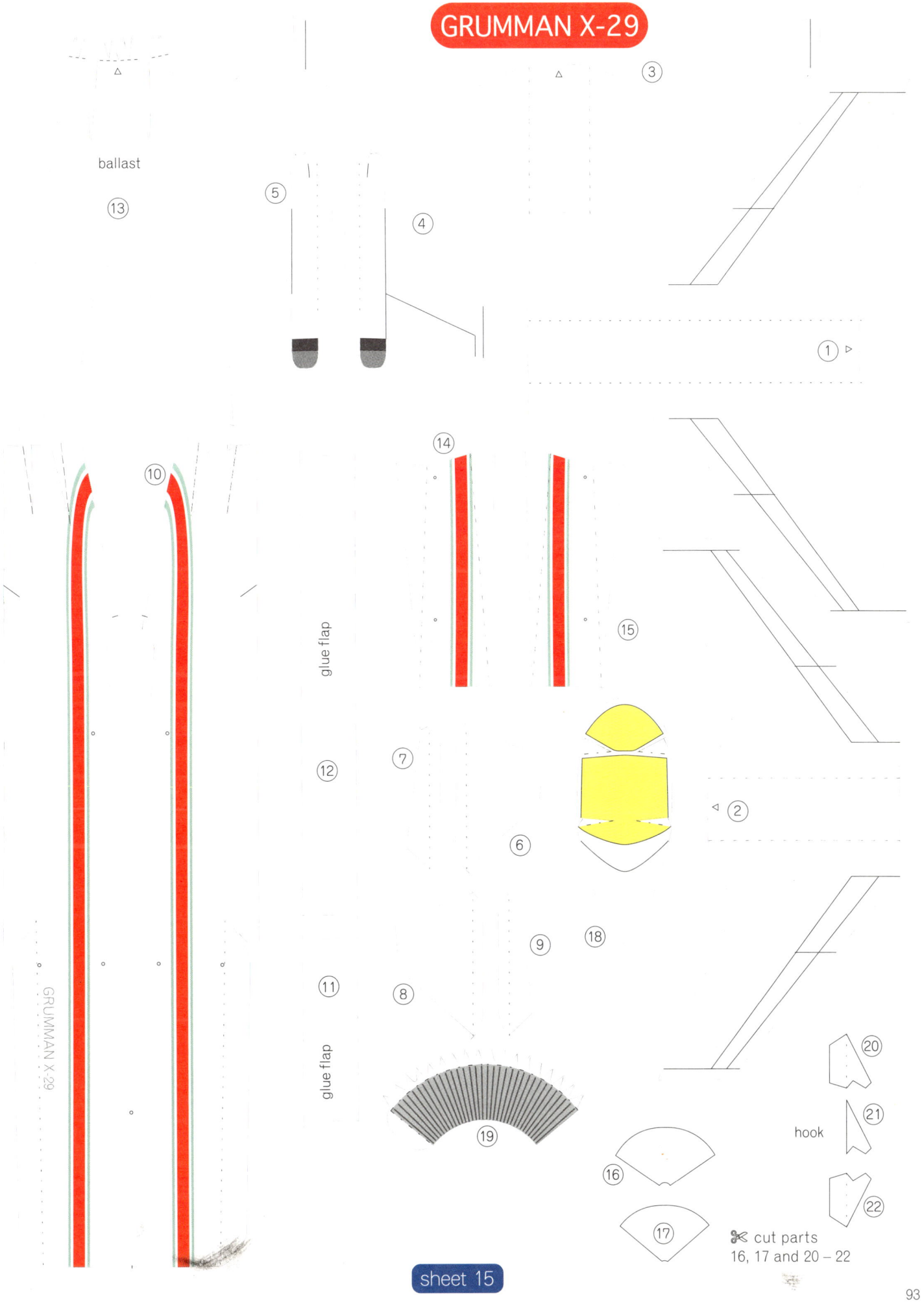

LOCKHEED F-117 NIGHTHAWK

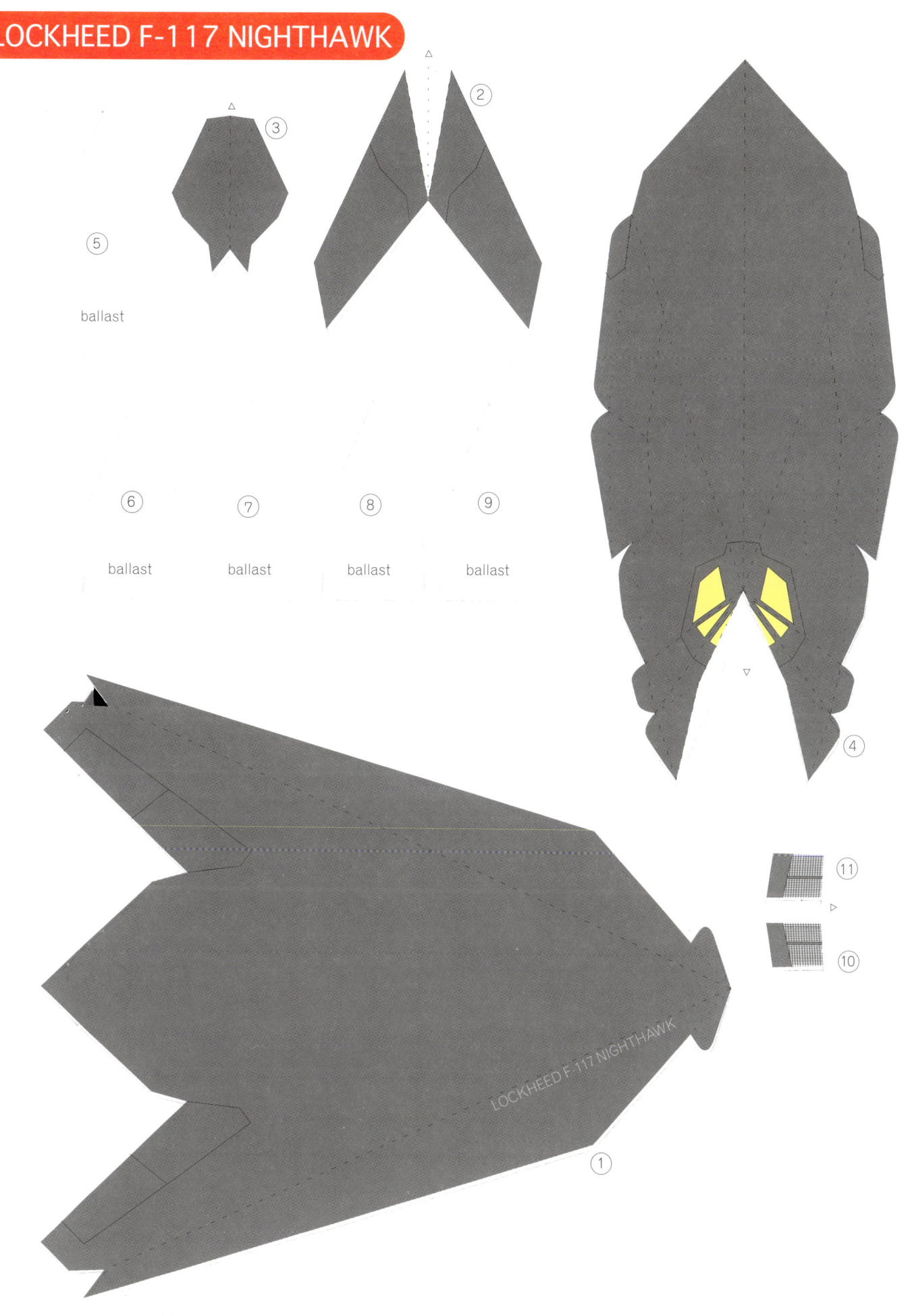

sheet 16